The Origami Artist's Bible

ASHLEY WOOD

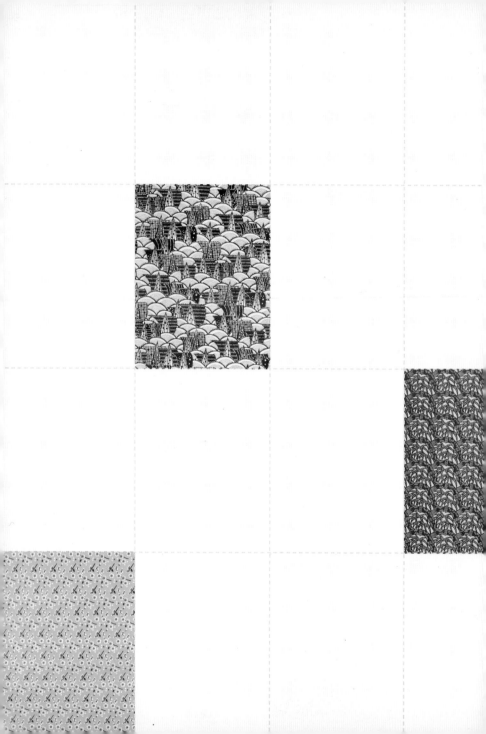

The Origami Artist's Bible

ASHLEY WOOD

CHARTWELL
BOOKS, INC.

Contents

A QUARTO BOOK

Published in 2009 by
CHARTWELL BOOKS, INC.
A division of BOOK SALES, INC.
276 Fifth Avenue Suite 206
New York, New York 10001
USA

Reprinted 2010
Copyright © 2009 Quarto Inc.

ISBN-13: 978-0-7858-2496-1
ISBN-10: 0-7858-2496-0

QUAR.OBI

This book was designed and
produced by
Quarto Publishing plc
The Old Brewery
6 Blundell Street
London N7 9BH

Project editor: Chloe Todd Fordham
Proofreader: Liz Dalby
Design and illustration: Jatin Mehta,
   Asha Madhavan, Mrityunjoy
   Burman, Santosh Goriwale
Photographer: Simon Pask
Design assistants: Jessica Wilson,
   Saffron Stocker

Art director: Caroline Guest

Creative director: Moira Clinch
Publisher: Paul Carslake

Printed by Midas Printing
International Limited, China
Color separation by Modern Age
Repro House Ltd, Hong Kong

Introduction

Origami transcends gender, culture, and language. It demands no prior learning and no complex equipment; it can be done at any age, by anyone; models can be large or small, useful or ornamental. You can fold a bus ticket or a sheet of gold leaf, but the sole requirement of origami is that you enjoy it.

I first began folding in an attempt to interest a class in Hiroshima, using the story of the paper crane (right). The resulting "Origami Club" was incredibly fun and I've been folding paper ever since. For me, folding a pattern from memory relieves boredom on journeys and allows me to relax and consider problems.

This book is the book I desperately needed in the Origami Club. Up front is a simple set of origami folds, illustrated with clear step-by-step diagrams, and three essential origami "bases" that are the starting point for the project models in the rest of the book. The models are arranged according to theme; some are complex, requiring patience and practice and some are suitable for total beginners. The difficulty rating, which ranges from one-star (for beginners) to five-stars (for advanced artists), will help you to pick a project suitable to your skill level. The bases and folding symbols are reproduced on a pull-out page at the back of the book so that you may refer to them while working.

Remember, origami is a pleasure not a punishment—there are no Origami Police! Fold for fun, use fabulous papers, and don't be afraid to alter the designs in this book or invent your own origami models.

Ashley Wood

A SHORT HISTORY OF ORIGAMI

Folding paper became widespread in Japan from the seventh century AD. At around the same time, the Moors brought paper folding to Spain. As Muslims, their designs could not be figurative or emblematic, so origami remained largely a practical craft until the fifteenth century, when cheaper mass-produced paper became available. In 1797, the first paper-folding book was published and the new art form was named Origami from *oru* (to fold) and *kami* (paper). In the 1930s, Akira Yoshizawa developed a system of arrows and patterns still used today to describe design instructions. Yoshizawa is seen as the grand master of origami. He created thousands of models in a lifelike, engaging style until his death in 2005. You will find his famous origami instructions on page 14, and on the pull-out page at the back of this book.

ORIGAMI TODAY

In recent times, the origami paper crane (page 71) has become a symbol of peace and is folded millions of times across the world. Engineers have used origami to solve complex problems, therapists have used it to rehabilitate damaged muscles, and many others have used it to meditate, concentrate, decorate, and entertain. In the future, origami will continue to evolve—and yet it will always stay rooted in tradition, a welcome link to the past.

The story of Sadako Sasaki

"I SHALL WRITE PEACE UPON YOUR WINGS, YOUR HEART AND YOU SHALL FLY AROUND THE WORLD SO THAT CHILDREN WILL NO LONGER HAVE TO DIE THIS WAY"—TRANSLATED HAIKU BY SADAKO SASAKI

Ten years after the nuclear bomb was dropped on Hiroshima on August 6, 1945, Sadako Sasaki (aged 12) was diagnosed with leukemia, and was hospitalized. One day, her best friend Chizuko Hamamoto visited her in hospital, and showed her how to fold a paper crane. "Anyone who folds 1000 paper cranes will be granted a wish," she told her. Sadako began to fold. She folded using scraps of wrapping paper from other patients, paper brought by Chizuko from school, and even medicine wrappings. When she died on October 25, 1955, Sadako had folded 644 cranes. Her friends folded the remaining 356, which were buried with her. In 1958, a statue of Sadako holding a golden crane was unveiled in the Hiroshima Peace Memorial. She has since become a focus of the Peace movement, and hundreds of Senbarazu (groups of 1000 cranes on strings) are sent from all over the world every day in her memory.

Paper types

However skilful the fold, or revolutionary the design, the main determining factor in the success of an origami model is the paper. Use these pages to help you pick the right paper for your designs, but above all, be bold and experiment.

KAMI PAPER

Kami origami paper is colored on one side and white on the other. Hundreds of different patterns and textured papers are available.

Specific use

Classic 6in (15cm) origami paper can be folded into almost anything. The benefit of this paper is that it is perfectly square.

Weight	Light
Creasing	This paper creases neatly, but can tear when large numbers of creases are made in a small area.
Durability	Average
Approx cost	$11 (£8) for 250 6in (15cm) sheets
Size	6in (15cm) square; 3in (7.5cm) square

TIP
Use the yucky colors in mixed packs to practice!

DUO PAPER

Classic duo paper is 6in (15cm) origami paper. Each side is a different color.

Specific use

This special type of origami paper is brilliant for designs where the "white" side of the paper is used as part of the design.

Weight	Light
Creasing	This paper creases neatly, but can tear when large numbers of creases are made in a small area.
Durability	Average
Approx cost	$14 (£10) per pack
Size	6in (15cm) square

FOIL PAPER

Foil paper can be paper-based or card-based and comes in a wide range of colors. It has one metallic side and one white.

Specific use

This paper is perfect for Christmas decorations.

Weight	Various
Creasing	Creases can cause unsightly white lines, so be gentle.
Durability	Average
Approx cost	$14 (£10) per pack
Size	Letter (A4) or 6in (15cm) square

> *TIP*
> Creasing heavily can cause the foil to rip; be gentle and *never* iron because it may melt!

WRAPPING PAPER

Wrapping paper is usually white on one side with a printed pattern on the other, but look out for luxury double-sided sheets and flocked or glittery papers.

Specific use

Use for large designs, gifts, and last-minute party decorations.

Weight	Light
Creasing	Creases can cause unsightly white lines, so be gentle.
Durability	Poor
Approx cost	Depends on the quality
Size	Rolls, packs, or sheets

> *TIP*
> Packs can't be used for large projects as the packaging creases will show.

PETAL PAPER

Petal paper is a classic 6in (15cm) origami paper with a flat color on one side and a variegated color on the other.

Specific use

This paper is specially designed for flowers. It has colors on both sides to make lovely blooms.

Weight	Light
Creasing	This paper creases neatly, but can tear when large numbers of creases are made in a small area.
Durability	Average
Approx cost	$14 (£10) per pack
Size	6in (15cm) square

CHIYOGAMI PAPER

Chiyogami paper is similar to Washi paper (not shown), but thinner and without the "cottony" feel.

Specific use

Use for intricate models where a traditional feel is desired.

Weight	Light
Creasing	This paper creases neatly, but can tear when large numbers of creases are made in a small area.
Durability	Average
Approx cost	$14 (£10) per pack
Size	6in (15cm) square; 3in (7.5cm) square; 8in x 10in (20cm x 25cm)

TIP
Set a budget before you go shopping; this paper is dangerously lovely!

PHOTOCOPYING PAPER

This is rectangular, smooth paper that comes in reams of 500 sheets and in several colors—more expensive single sheets are available in many more patterns and colors.

Specific use

This paper is just right for practicing; it's cheap, regularly sized and medium weight. Use it to amuse children, or to build big modular projects.

Weight	Medium
Creasing	Holds creases well
Durability	Average
Approx cost	$6 (£3.50) for a ream (500 sheets)
Size	Letter (A4)

TIP
When you need to know which side of the paper is which as you fold, scribble on one side of the paper before you start to practice.

SCRAP PAPER

This could be anything from a receipt to an off-cut of very expensive paper.

Specific use

Keep all your pretty scraps and use them for practice, fold in a queue or on the bus, do something interesting with your junk mail… the possibilities are endless!

Weight	Various
Creasing	Various
Durability	Various
Approx cost	Nothing
Size	Various

TIP
Use scrap paper to distract curious pets from your works in progress—and try not to fold important documents!

CHINESE HANDMADE

Semi-transparent with fibers running through it, this special paper comes in hundreds of color variations.

Specific use

Use where transparency or texture is an advantage.

Weight	Various
Creasing	Fibers do not crease well
Durability	Average
Approx cost	$2 (£1.50) per A2 sheet
Size	Letter (A4) A3, and A2

NAPKINS

Squares of fabric or tissue. Paper napkins come in a huge variety of colors and patterns.

Specific use

Table decoration and spillage control.

Weight	Heavy
Creasing	Creases can be made loose or sharp
Durability	Fabric can be reused
Approx cost	Depends on quality
Size	14in (33cm) or 18in (44cm) squares

CARDSTOCK

Squares of thin card used in scrapbooking and cardmaking. They come in a variety of colors and patterns.

Specific use

Particularly useful for boxes and, surprisingly, for boats as it is reasonably watertight.

Weight	Heavy
Creasing	Holds creases well
Durability	Good
Approx cost	$1 (£0.50) per sheet
Size	12in (30cm) and 6in (15cm) square

TIP
For crisp folds use an iron without steam (for paper napkins) or steam and starch (for fabric napkins).

TIP
Chinese handmade paper crumples very easily so use an iron with the steam switched off to smooth it.

TIP
Buy cardstock in packs and use less attractive sheets to practice with. Cardstock has different characteristics to photocopying paper.

This specialist branch of origami is prevalent in every country where paper money is printed but it is especially popular in North America. This may be because the American dollar bill is of a unique height–width ratio, 3:7, and is one of the few widely available notes with a small enough denomination to fold with impunity.

Another reason may be that the design of the dollar bill has not changed since 1963. Money folding designs are created to make use of the words and pictures on the note, and this longevity means there are many more designs available.

GIs used to fold money during the Second World War, creating a number of salacious designs—and one for a bowtie with the President's face in the knot. Magicians and bartenders then took up the art form. Customers of a quiet bar once asked the bartender to fold their change as a gift to placate their wives at home.

PAPER MONEY

Paper money models are usually made up with rectangular US dollar bills because few currencies have a note of this small a denomination.

Specific use
There's a whole branch of origami dedicated to folding dollar bills—most use the pictures on the bill to form part of the design.

Weight	Medium
Creasing	Holds creases well
Durability	Excellent
Approx cost	$1 each, of course!
Size	US dollar only

TIP
Iron on a high heat with plenty of steam to kill germs before you fold.

Essential origami folds

Origami is the art of folding. Each model, regardless of complexity, is made from two folds: the valley fold and the mountain fold. Ensuring each crease is precise guarantees an attractive final product.

See also
You will find all the origami symbols on the pull-out page at the back of the book.

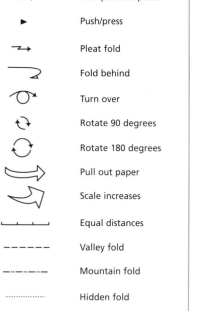

	Direction paper moves
	Fold and unfold again
	Fold and unfold again
	Repeat once
	Repeat three times
	Fold point to point
	Push/press
	Pleat fold
	Fold behind
	Turn over
	Rotate 90 degrees
	Rotate 180 degrees
	Pull out paper
	Scale increases
	Equal distances
	Valley fold
	Mountain fold
	Hidden fold
	Existing crease
	Fold with feeling

VALLEY FOLD

This fold is made with the paper laid flat on the table. The arrow shows the direction of paper movement; it is usually folded to a specific point, edge, or crease.

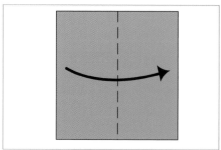

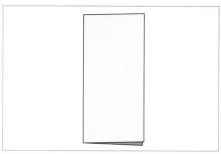

VALLEY FOLD AND UNFOLD

Fold the paper as before, and then unfold in the direction of the arrow. The thin line in the second diagram shows the existence of a pre-crease; this fold can be used later on in the directions to form a structure.

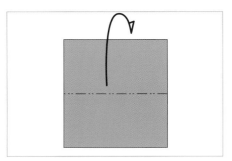 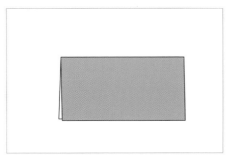

MOUNTAIN FOLD

The paper is folded underneath—it must either be held in the air, or turned over and valley folded as before. The arrowhead is different from the valley fold, as is the line pattern.

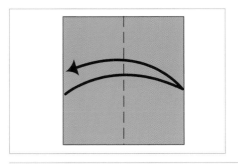 

MOUNTAIN FOLD AND UNFOLD

Fold the paper as before, and then unfold again. This arrow seems very complex in shape, but the fold is simple and forms an upward pointing pre-crease.

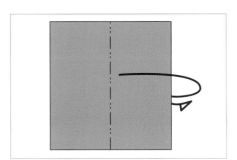 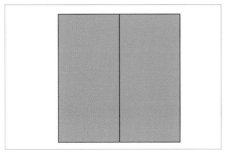

REPEAT FOLD

This arrow indicates that the fold in the diagram should be repeated. The notches on the arrow indicate the number of repeats. Always check the next diagram in a sequence if in doubt.

PLEAT FOLD

This sequence of valley and mountain folds causes the upper layer of paper to pass over the lower layer, forming three layers of paper in one section. Check the fold symbols on the pull-out flap to ensure that you are pleating in the correct direction.

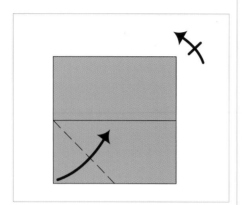

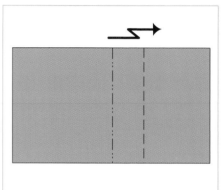

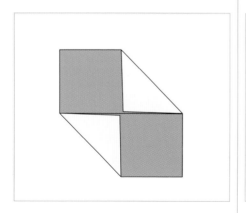

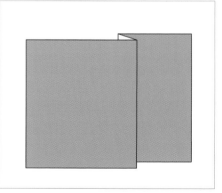

See also

The origami symbols are listed on the pull-out page at the back of the book, for easy reference as you fold.

DIVIDING INTO THIRDS

Start with a square folded in half. Fold the bottom right corner to the top center (1). Turn over (2). Fold the top right corner to where the two raw edges meet (3). Unfold (4). The paper is in one third and two thirds (5).

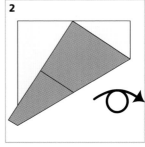

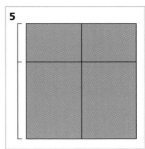

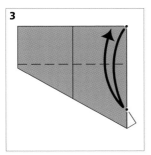

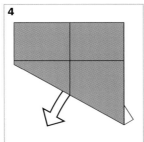

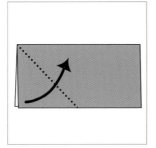

HIDDEN FOLDS

Occasionally, folds are made using layers of paper hidden inside the model. In this case, a dotted line indicates where the fold takes place.

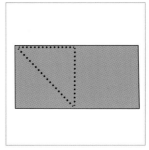

PULL OUT PAPER

Some paper is released from within or underneath the model. Often, some degree of unfolding is necessary—but never force the paper as it is likely to tear.

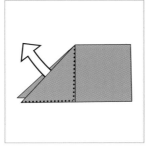

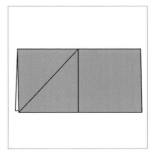

INSIDE REVERSE

The inside reverse technique converts a section of the paper from mountain fold to valley fold.

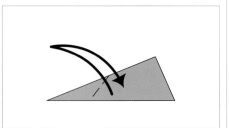

1 Make a pre-crease where the reverse fold will be.

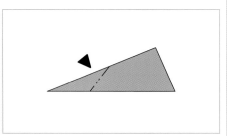

2 Press the end of the paper gently, so that it reverses direction, re-creasing the folds made in step 1 as mountain folds.

3 The completed reverse fold. Ensure you check what the finished fold should look like before creating the creases in step 1.

OUTSIDE REVERSE

The outside reverse fold converts a section of paper from valley fold to mountain fold. Quite often this technique is used to create feet or beaks, but it has many other uses.

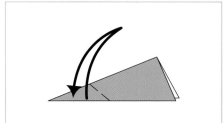

1 Make a pre-crease where the reverse fold will be.

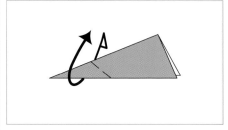

2 Peel apart the end of the paper, wrapping it around so that it reverses direction, re-creasing the folds made in step 1 as valley folds.

3 The completed reverse fold. Ensure you check what the finished fold should look like before creating the creases in step 1.

INSIDE CRIMP

Crimps allow you to create a change in angle in a strip or pointed flap of paper. Multiple crimps can be used to suggest a curve in straight paper.

OUTSIDE CRIMP

This can be used in the same way as the inside crimp but take care as the outside crimp has a "jagged" finish.

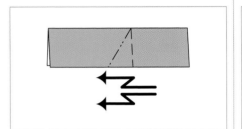

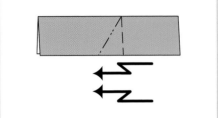

1 The paper on the right will be folded under the paper on the left. The pattern of creases is identical on the layer underneath.

1 The paper on the right will be folded over the paper on the left. The pattern of creases is identical on the layer underneath.

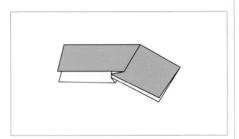

2 Form the creases carefully on both sides of the paper. Use pre-creases for precision.

2 Form the creases carefully on both sides of the paper. Use pre-creases for precision.

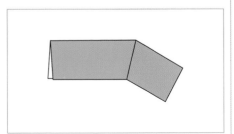

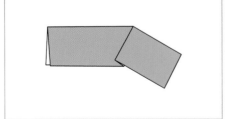

3 Press the completed crimp flat from both sides. This crimp creates a smooth effect.

3 Press the completed crimp flat from both sides. This crimp creates a flap of paper to the left.

Origami bases

See also
Swan, page 68
Cat, page 78

When origami began to be analyzed in the early part of the last century, it came to light that several designs began with an identical sequence of folds. These came to be known as "bases" and were given names that usually reflected a design common to them. Thus, a kite base can be made into a kite, and so forth. One exception is the preliminary base, so-called because it is a starting point for many different designs. A thorough grounding in the following three traditional bases will help you toward success in origami, and enable you to attempt all of the projects in this book.

KITE BASE

This is a very simple base, but it is used in a wide range of projects and is very flexible.

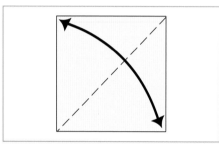

1 Fold paper diagonally in half. Remember that this is the basis of your design, and any small inaccuracy will be amplified in the final model.

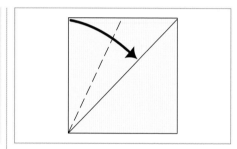

2 Fold an edge in, to lie along the center crease. Lift the opposite side of the paper, and push the edge tight up against the previous fold.

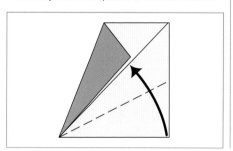

3 Fold in the remaining edge to lie along the center crease.

4 The completed kite base. Many designs call for the base to be folded in half at this point.

REMINDERS OF THE BASE DIAGRAMS ARE ON THE PULL-OUT PAGE AT THE BACK OF THE BOOK.

PRELIMINARY BASE

Called the preliminary base because it forms the first half of the bird base (not shown), this base is used widely in origami. It is more complex than the kite base, and must be folded carefully.

See also

Star pot, page 38
Crane, page 71

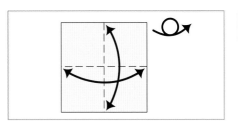

1 Fold paper horizontally and vertically in half—remember that this is the basis of your design, and any small inaccuracy will be amplified in the final model. Unfold. Turn over.

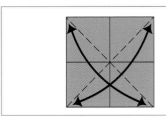

2 Fold paper diagonally in half in both directions. Unfold.

3 Fold the paper in half horizontally, using the step 1 crease. Hold the two short sides, and bring them down and to the middle, so that all the corners of the paper are together at the bottom.

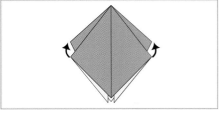

4 Flatten the base, bringing the two corners on each side together, and ensuring that all the points meet neatly at the bottom of the base.

5 The completed preliminary base. Note that the color inside is facing upward in step 1. When moving on from this point, ensure you have the base facing in the right direction at each stage of folding.

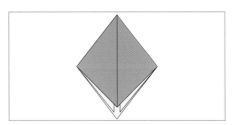

WATERBOMB BASE

This base is essentially the opposite of the preliminary base—it has the same folds, but is formed in a different way, and begins with the paper face up.

See also
Rabbit, page 89

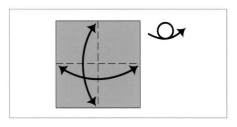

1 Fold paper horizontally and vertically in half. Remember that this is the basis of your design, and any small inaccuracy will be amplified in the final model. Unfold. Turn over.

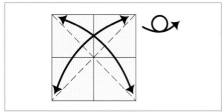

2 Fold paper diagonally in half in both directions. Unfold. Turn over.

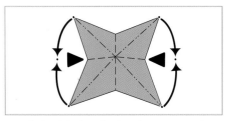

3 Push the sides in, allowing the center to rise up, and the sides to come together.

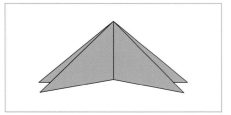

4 Flatten the base bringing the two corners to each side together, ensuring all the points meet neatly at the bottom of the base. Note that the color outside is facing upward in step 1.

Cutting your paper

To make the majority of the projects in this book, you will need to cut your paper to very specific sizes—often perfect squares, equilateral triangles, and even hexagons.

SQUARE FROM RECTANGLE

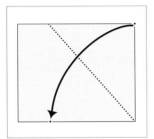 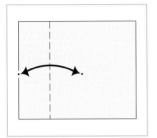 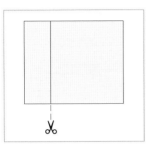

1 Fold a diagonal and mark the top edge of the fold with a small crease. Unfold.

2 Fold over the edge of the paper at the crease mark. Crease the whole fold. Unfold.

3 Cut off the end of the paper to leave a square.

RECTANGLE FROM SQUARE

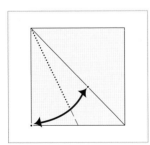 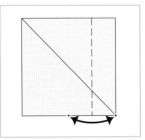 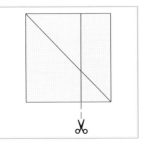

1 Fold a square in half diagonally then fold one side to lie along the crease. Pinch where the edge folds. Unfold.

2 Fold in the edge of the opposite side so that it meets the pinch mark. Crease firmly. Unfold.

3 Cut off the end of the paper. This will leave a rectangle of roughly letter-size (A4) proportions.

TRIANGLE FROM RECTANGLE

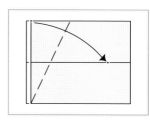

1 Pre-crease the midpoint horizontally, then fold dot to dot.

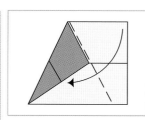

2 Fold across.

3 Unfold.

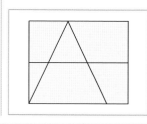

4 Cut off the excess paper to leave an equilateral triangle.

HEXAGON FROM SQUARE

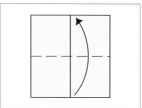

1 Pre-crease a horizontal midpoint, then fold the bottom edge to the top.

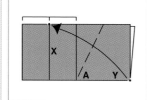

2 Pinch crease X. Fold corner Y to touch crease X, so that this new crease starts exactly at A.

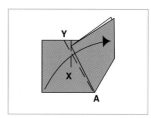

3 Fold across.

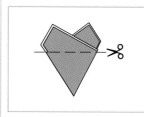

4 Cut off the excess paper and open the triangle.

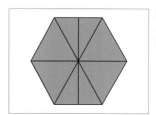

5 The completed hexagon.

Origami tools

Useful tools for the creation of attractive origami are shown here—you will find other useful items as you practice.

Hands: Take care of them! Use hand cream to offset frequent washing.

Scissors: Use a sharp pair, kept just for paper.

Pens and pencils: Use to mark divisions or add facial features to your designs.

Ruler: Clean carefully before you use.

Tweezers: Useful for miniature models with tiny creases.

Guillotine: Use to cut wrapping paper into precise squares.

Glue: Paper glue can be used to hold together two-part structures.

Baby wipes: Use for cleaning the work surface and your hands often.

Hints and tips

Origami is a precise art, relying on accurate folding; but it is also an outlet for creativity. Below are some hints for successful folding.

❑ Clean your hands! Paper picks up natural oils from your fingers.

❑ Fold on a surface to increase precision.

❑ Use a clean, smooth surface—bumps and grit damage delicate paper.

❑ Fold away from your body, using valley folds wherever possible.

❑ For tiny creases use tweezers rather than your fingers.

❑ Alter existing designs by experimenting with different paper shapes and angles.

THE PROJECTS

he projects are collected into sections according to their form
nd function; you can set children loose on a group of models
hat fly or move, fold a napkin for a dinner party, or create an
rigami container or Christmas decoration. Refer to the pull-out
age at the back of the book as you work through the projects
nd, with a little practice, you will be able to make any of the
nodels in this book—be bold and have a go!

THE SELECTOR

CONTAINERS

33–34 GIFT ENVELOPE

35–36 FOLDED ENVELOPE

37 FOLDED ENVELOPE 2

38–39 STAR POT

40–42 JAPANESE BOX

43–45 CIRCULAR DISH

46–47 FUSE BOX

48–49 TWISTED DISH

50–52 INCENSE BURNER

54–55 HEXAGONAL BOX

NAPKINS

57–59 WATER LILY

60–61 SAIL

62–63 FAN

64–65 FLAME

ANIMALS AND FLOWERS

66–67 COCKADE

68–69 SWAN

71–73 CRANE

74–75 BUTTERFLY

76–77 FOX

78–79 CAT

81–82 TULIP

83–85 FROG

86–88 ROOSTER

89–91 RABBIT

93–97 TORTOISE

98–103 DAFFODIL

CHILDREN'S ORIGAMI

104–108 CORGI

109–117 VASE OF FLOWERS

119–121 ELEPHANT PLANE

122–123 BANGER

124–129 PARROT

130–131 PIRATE'S HAT

132–133 LOOPING GLIDER

134–135 FLAPPING BIRD

136–137 ROWING BOAT

138–139 PUZZLE

140–141 BARKING DOG

142–143 FLYING SAUCER

144–145 WOODPECKER

146–147 PINWHEEL

148–151 GHOST

153–155 BAUBLE

156–157 FOUR-PIECE STAR

158–159 PLACECARD

160–161 SIX-POINT STAR

162–163 ANGEL

FOLDER'S HEAVEN

164–166 MAN IN THE MOON

169–171 POP-UP BOX

172–173 SNAP HEXAHEDRON

174–175 MODULAR BALL

176–177 PAPER MOSAIC

178–181 STRETCH WALL

182–184 CUBE

185–186 UN-UNFOLDABLE BOX

CONTAINERS

Containers make up the most useful branch of origami and, like all paper folding designs, they are elegant and attractive to look at. Here there is a wide selection—from envelopes and simple dishes to complex and beautiful gift boxes. The dishes in this chapter can be made as gifts from beautiful papers in colors to suit your taste. It is also worth experimenting with different types of paper too; some handmade papers have fantastic textures, and will create amazing results.

Gift envelope

SKILL LEVEL

You will need

❏ Sheet of wrapping paper

THIS GIFT ENVELOPE IS PERFECT FOR WRAPPING CDS (AS SHOWN HERE), DVDS, AND COMPUTER GAMES, OR YOU COULD USE IT TO HOLD A PARTICULARLY BULKY HANDMADE CARD. IT IS NOT SUITABLE FOR POSTING, BUT YOU COULD USE A HANDMADE BUTTON AS AN OLD-FASHIONED SEAL.

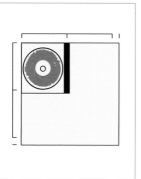

1 Place the CD in a corner of the paper. Measure twice the height and twice the width of the CD, then add a little extra. Trim the paper to these dimensions.

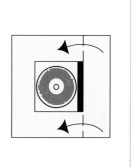

2 Place the CD approximately in the center of the paper, square to the edges. Fold in the right-hand edge.

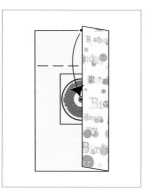

3 Fold down the top edge.

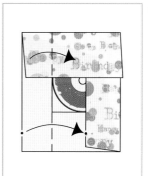

4 Fold in the left edge.

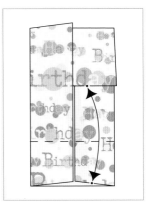

5 Fold and unfold the bottom edge.

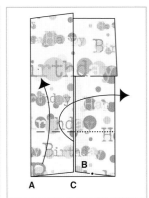

6 Valley-fold A up the left-hand edge. Open B...

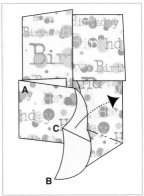

7 ...and push C deep inside, making a mountain fold across the bottom.

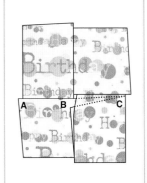

8 Crease firmly to hold the layers together.

Why not start with the gift envelope off-center to create enough space to tuck a card in the folds?

Folded envelope 1

SKILL LEVEL

You will need

❒ 12in (30cm) square of light- or medium-weight paper creased vertically down the middle

THIS ENVELOPE COULD BE SENT THROUGH THE POST IF YOU USE STRONG PAPER AND SOME DOUBLE-SIDED TAPE TO SEAL IT—BUT IT'S ALSO A VERY ATTRACTIVE WAY OF PRESENTING A HANDMADE CARD.

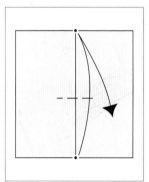

1 Fold the bottom edge up to the top and press it flat in the middle to find the mid-point of the square.

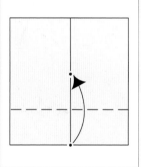

2 Fold the bottom edge up to the center.

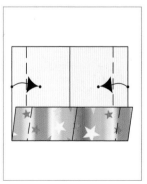

3 Fold in the sides.

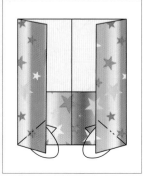

4 Fold the loose corners behind at the bottom.

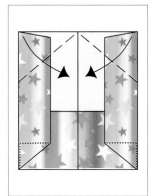

5 Fold the top corners into the center vertical crease.

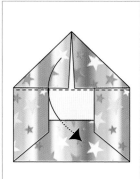

6 Crease across the base of the top triangles, tucking them inside the pocket. This locks the envelope shut.

Envelopes can be made from wrapping paper, to match a wrapped gift, or from handmade paper for a luxurious effect.

Folded envelope 2

SKILL LEVEL

You will need

☐ 12in (30cm) square of light- or medium-weight paper

THIS IS A MORE INTRICATE ENVELOPE, THAT IS NOT REALLY STURDY ENOUGH TO GO THROUGH THE POST—HOWEVER, IT IS VERY ATTRACTIVE, PARTICULARLY WHEN MADE FROM STRIPED PAPER.

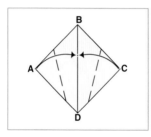

1 Crease a line (BD). Unfold. Fold corners A and C onto the crease, making sure the new creases don't meet corner D.

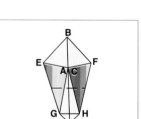

2 Crease and unfold G to H.

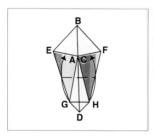

3 Fold up D so that corner G lies on edge EA and corner H on CF.

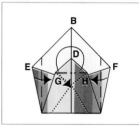

4 Fold D inside, tucking it behind A and C; this locks G and H flat. Fold in E and F hard against edges G and H.

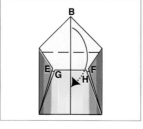

5 Slide B under edge GH and push it until it will not go any further. Flatten and crease.

6 The envelope is complete. To unlock it, pull out corner B.

Star pot

See also
Preliminary base,
page 21

SKILL LEVEL

You will need

❏ Preliminary base from 8in (20cm) square of medium-weight paper

THIS TRADITIONAL AND ELEGANT DESIGN MAKES USE OF SQUASH FOLDS. IF YOU USE PAPER WITH DIFFERENT COLORS ON EITHER SIDE, THE STAR WILL BE A DIFFERENT COLOR THAN THE BOX. THE OPENING OF THE BOX WHEN IT IS FINISHED PROVIDES A STRIKING CLIMAX TO THE SEQUENCE.

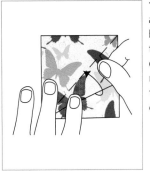

1 Start with a preliminary base with the open end down. Fold a raw-edged flap to the center crease.

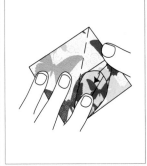

2 Lift the flap back toward you and make a squash-fold, separating the layers evenly to either side.

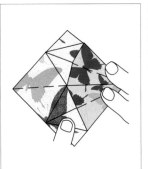

3 Turn the paper around and repeat with the opposite flap.

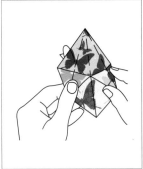

4 Hold the paper in the air and mountain fold the outer half of the kite shape, tucking the flaps inside. Repeat with the three remaining flaps.

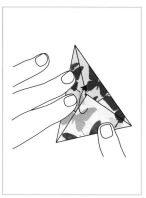

5 Make a firm horizontal crease, joining the base of the two small triangles.

6 Unfold and swing the point at the top downward as far as it will comfortably go. Repeat on the flap on the other side.

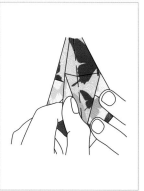

7 Fold the left-hand flap to the right and swing the upper point downward as far as it will go.

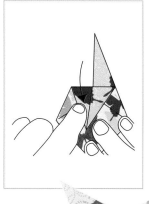

8 Fold the right flap to the left and repeat for the remaining point.

9 Turn the paper upside down, place a finger inside the opening, and start to flatten the base into a neat square. Sharpen the creases around the base to complete.

The color on the inside of the base will end up on the inside of the box. Use paper with contrasting colored sides for the best effect.

Japanese box

SKILL LEVEL

You will need

☐ 12in x 18in (30cm x 45cm) sheet of medium- or heavy-weight paper

THIS TRADITIONAL DESIGN IS MORE OF A BOWL THAN A BOX, BUT IT MAKES UP FOR ITS LACK OF LID WITH AN ELEGANT SIMPLICITY OF DESIGN. IT IS VERY STURDY AND CAN BE MADE IN A HURRY FOR LAST-MINUTE PARTY SNACKS.

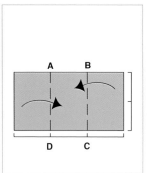

1 Divide the paper into thirds, first folding BC across to the left, then folding AD across on top to the right.

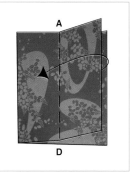

2 Fold AD back to the left edge.

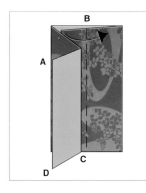

3 Pull out edge BC from under AD and fold it back to the right.

4 Unfold BC so that it meets and covers AD.

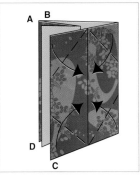

5 Turn in the four corners, with the ones at B and C being single layers.

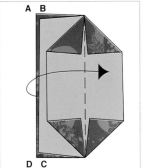

6 Fold BC back over to the right to meet the right-hand edge.

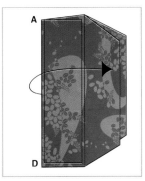

7 Unfold AD over to the right.

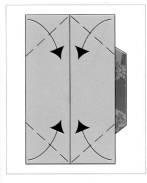

8 Turn in the four corners to meet the center crease.

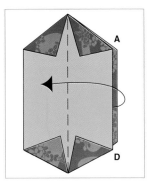

9 Fold AD back over to the left.

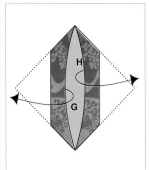

10 The paper is now symmetrical. Pull open the slit at G and H...

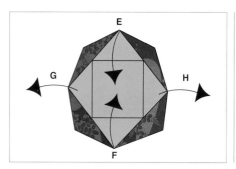

11 ...opening up the box. Continue to pull so that, as G and H separate, E and F come together in the middle...

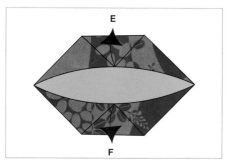

12 ...like this. Open up EF a little to complete the box.

This box works best with dramatic colors to maximize the impact of its simple design.

Circular dish

SKILL LEVEL

You will need

☐ 12in (30cm) square of paper with a pattern on both sides

THIS IS A VERY UNUSUAL DESIGN—IT IS ONE OF THE FEW CIRCULAR ORIGAMI PATTERNS, AND WILL MAKE A GREAT CENTERPIECE AT A PARTY. HOWEVER YOU WILL NEED TO USE HEAVY-WEIGHT PAPER OR CARD IF YOU WISH TO USE IT TO HOLD YOUR PARTY SNACKS!

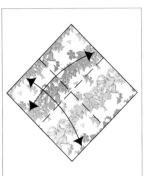

1 Valley fold in half horizontally and vertically, to make four squares. Unfold each crease.

2 Mountain fold each diagonal. Unfold.

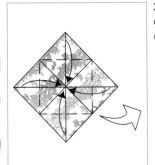

3 Fold the corners to the center.

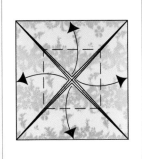

4 Fold the corners back out to the edge.

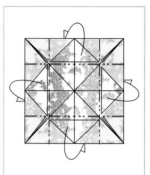

5 Crease and unfold four mountain folds as shown. (It is probably easier to make valley folds by turning the paper over.)

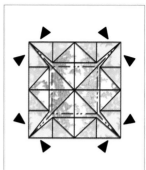

6 Make short mountain diagonals. Pinch the edges near the corners...

7 ...to raise a table shape in the center. Push down on the central point while pushing the edges of the "table" toward the center...

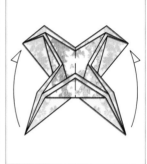

8 ...like this. Note the X shape of the paper. Flatten the X shape with two points on either side.

9 Reverse-fold the front corners inside.

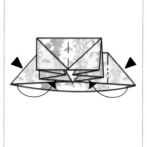

10 Repeat for the back corners.

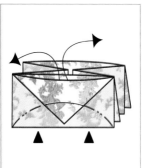

11 Push the bottom edge upward with a curved crease, so that the top edges of the pocket separate in a curved shape.

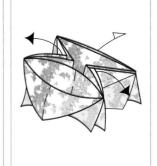

12 Repeat on the other three sides. The dish is now complete. Neaten the interior edges to make an attractive star-shaped central pocket.

Look for double-sided wrapping paper for these boxes—or use two sheets of mulberry paper glued together.

Fuse box

SKILL LEVEL

You will need

☐ Eight sheets of 6in (15cm) square light- or medium-weight paper

TOMOKO FUSE CAUSED A MINOR REVOLUTION IN ORIGAMI WHEN SHE UNVEILED HER SYSTEM FOR MAKING BOXES FROM SEVERAL SHEETS OF PAPER. THIS IS ONE OF THE SIMPLEST OF HER REPERTOIRE, AND A CLASSIC OF ECONOMY AND EFFICIENCY.

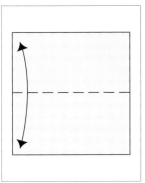

1 Start with a square, lighter side upward, and crease it in half.

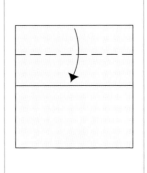

2 Fold the top edge to the center crease. Turn the paper over.

3 Fold in half from side to side, crease, and unfold. Turn the paper over again.

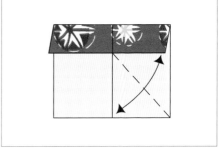

4 Crease the lower right diagonal and unfold.

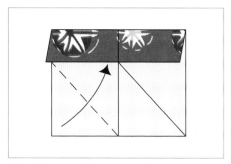

5 Fold the lower left corner to the center.

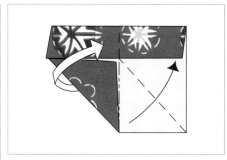

6 Crease as shown. Pinch the upper third of the center crease into a valley.

7 Swing the triangular flap downward to finish the unit. Make three more in the same way.

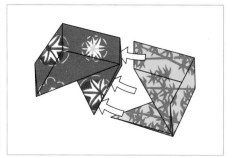

8 Arrange two units as shown and slide them partially into each other. Repeat with another two units. Slide in each pair, little by little, until they are tight together to form a box shape.

You may feel that you need an extra pair of hands toward the end of this project, but persevere—the result is delightful, and useful too.

Twisted dish

SKILL LEVEL

You will need

☐ 12in (30cm) square of light- or medium-weight paper

THIS DISH USES A SIMPLE LOCKING TECHNIQUE TO FORM THE SIDES. THE CREASES ARE PREPARED IN ADVANCE, A TECHNIQUE KNOWN AS "PRE-CREASING." YOU SHOULD MAKE SURE ALL PRE-CREASING IS ACCURATE. FOLD THE CREASES IN REVERSE TO CREATE A DISH THAT "TWISTS" THE OTHER WAY.

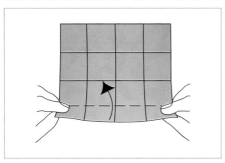

1 Divide a square into sixteen smaller squares. Fold the nearest edge over to the center crease.

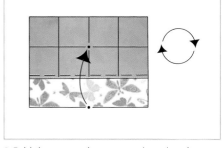

2 Fold the same edge over again, using the halfway crease. Rotate the paper 180 degrees.

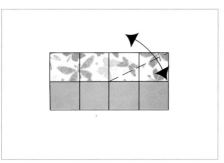

3 Make a crease that joins the top right outside corner with the center of your paper.

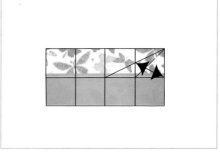

4 Unfold. Then fold the short raw edges on the right to meet the most recent crease made.

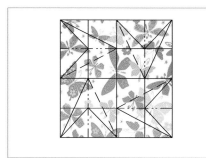

5 Open the paper out and repeat steps 1 through 4 on the three other edges. Unfold once more, and turn the paper over.

6 Pinch together one of the "darts" created in steps 1–5 and lock into place by folding the small triangle behind.

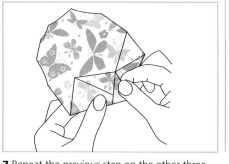

7 Repeat the previous step on the other three corners. Take care with the final corner.

Using paper with a pattern on one side and a plain color on the other mimics the design of china bowls.

Incense burner

SKILL LEVEL

You will need

☐ 8in (20cm) square of medium-weight paper spray-mounted with aluminum foil

THE REVEREND PHILIP SHEN OF HONG KONG SPECIALIZES IN CREATING GEOMETRIC DESIGNS THAT COLLAPSE INTO SHAPE FROM A CAREFULLY LAID-OUT PATTERN OF PRE-CREASES. USING FOIL-COVERED PAPER REDUCES THE RISK OF FIRE, BUT YOU SHOULD NOT LEAVE THIS DESIGN UNATTENDED.

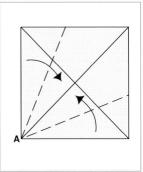

1 Fold the paper across the diagonals to make two creases. Fold the two edges meeting at A to the center crease.

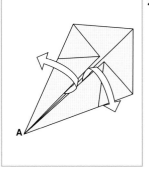

2 Unfold.

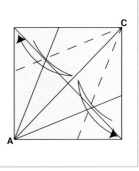

3 Repeat with the other two edges meeting at C.

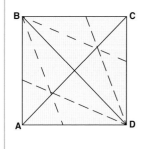

4 Repeat with the two edges meeting at B, then those meeting at D.

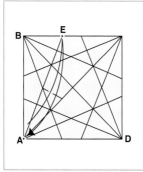

5 Fold A to E—E being at the end of the upper crease made in step 1. Crease only where shown.

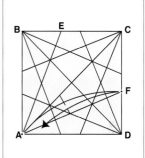

6 Repeat, folding A to F—F being at the end of the lower crease made in step 1.

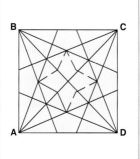

7 Repeat for B, C, and D, making six more short creases.

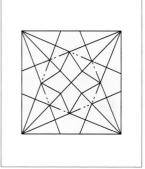

8 Re-crease the octagon with mountain creases.

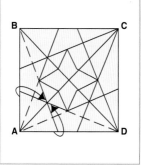

9 Fold in the creases as shown.

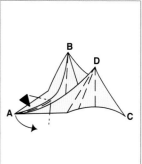

10 Reverse A along existing creases...

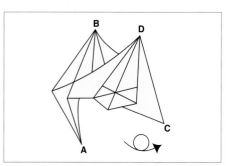

11 ...like this. Turn over.

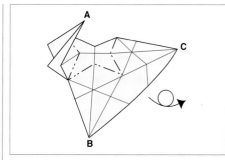

12 Turn back over and repeat steps 9–12 with B, C, and D, forming three more legs.

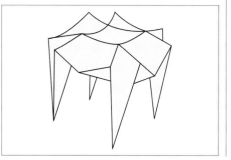

13 Strengthen the inner star shape with mountain creases.

Although this is made using foil, not paper, it should never be left alone while burning.

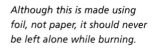

Hexagonal box

SKILL LEVEL

You will need

- ☐ 10½in x 8in (26.5cm x 20.5cm) strip of solid colored paper
- ☐ 11in x 4in (27.5cm x 10cm) strip of patterned paper

THESE BEAUTIFUL BOXES CAN BE MADE ENTIRELY WITHOUT GLUE—SEE IF YOU CAN WORK OUT HOW! IF YOU WISH THE BOX TO HOLD A HEAVY GIFT, USE CARDBOARD FOR THE BOTTOM OF IT.

THE BOX

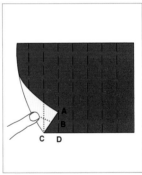

1 Fold the patterned paper into eight equal parts, using all valley folds. Fold point A up to lie on crease D. Crease firmly from point C up to crease B.

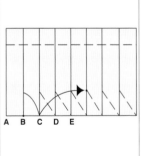

2 Continue to crease all the sections across the bottom of the paper. Fold down a 1in (2cm) strip at the top of the paper.

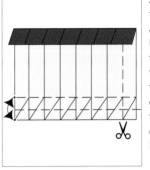

3 Crease along the top of the angled creases. Unfold. Fold the bottom of the paper to the previous crease. Cut off this strip. Cut off the right hand eighth.

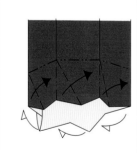

4 Form a tube and glue the two end panels, one on top of the other. Fold the end pieces as shown, and glue them together.

THE LID

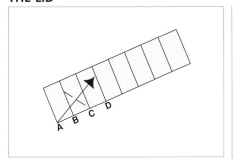

5 Fold the strip of colored paper into eight sections and fold point A up to crease D. Make a crease between point C and line B.

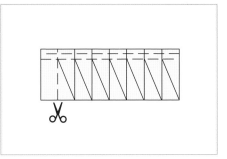

6 Crease along the top of the angled creases. Fold the bottom of the paper to the previous crease. Cut off the right hand eighth.

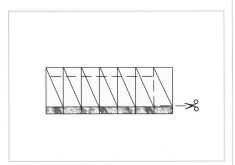

7 Fold a strip ½in (1.5cm) along the paper. Cut off this strip, plus the end panel.

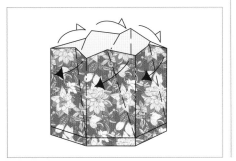

8 Form a tube. Glue the extra strip inside the fold at the bottom. Fold to form a rosette.

The box can be made in a different size. Just alter the size of the paper strips you begin with.

NAPKINS

Napkin folding is perhaps the best-known variation of origami. It is very simple, but effective when coupled with attractive place settings. Unlike other origami, it is most often used in a commercial setting; in restaurants or by caterers at large events. Paper napkins are used in other papercraft techniques, such as découpage, and come in thousands of designs.

Water lily

SKILL LEVEL

THIS IS THE FULL VERSION OF A SPECTACULAR NAPKIN FOLD SOMETIMES SEEN IN RESTAURANTS. A SIMPLE SERIES OF FOLDS IS GRADUALLY OPENED UP AND TRANSFORMED INTO THE BEAUTIFUL COMPLETED DESIGN—IT IS ALMOST LIKE MAGIC. USE A PAPER NAPKIN; FABRIC NAPKINS WILL NOT FORM THIS SHAPE.

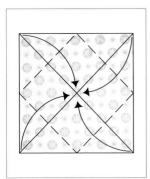

1 Fold the corners to the center.

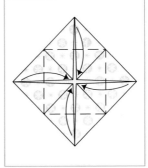

2 Again, fold the corners to the center.

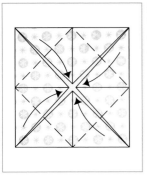

3 Once again, fold the corners to the center.

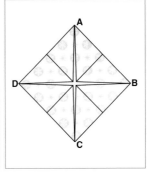

4 Note ABCD. Turn over.

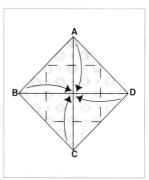

5 Yet again, fold the corners to the center.

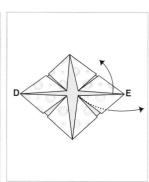

6 Note E. Hold all the layers flat and pull out corner A, mentioned in step 4.

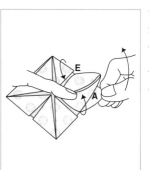

7 Hold as shown. Pull A forcibly upward, so that it unpeels around E...

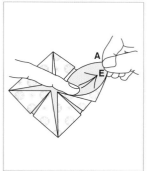

8 ...like this. Repeat with B, C, and D, keeping hold of the center.

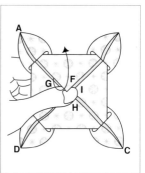

9 Turn over. Note FGHI. Lift F...

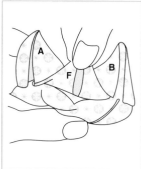

10 ...and pull it up between A and B, as far as it will go.

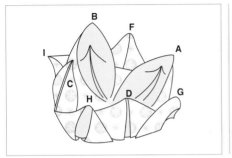

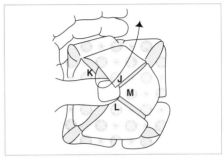

11 Repeat with G, H, and I, still keeping hold of the center.

12 Turn over. Note JKLM. Lift J and pull it up in front of A. Repeat with K, L, and M.

These beautiful napkins are deceptively intricate—just don't tell anyone how simple they really are!

Sail

You will need

❏ 13in (33cm) square paper napkin with a picture on one face

USE THIS LOVELY SHAPE IN A SOLID COLOR FOR A SIMPLE, STYLISH LOOK, BUT THIS FORM IS EQUALLY GOOD FOR DISPLAYING PICTORIAL NAPKINS. CHILDREN'S PARTY NAPKINS ARE PARTICULARLY SUITABLE AS THIS DESIGN IS EASY TO UNFOLD IN CASE OF SPILLAGES!

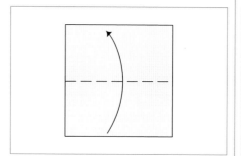

1 Fold the bottom edge up to the top.

2 Fold down the top right-hand corner.

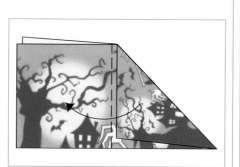

3 Fold the bottom-right corner across to the left edge.

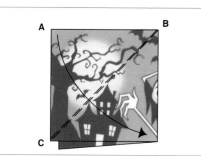

4 Fold corner A downward. Note B and C.

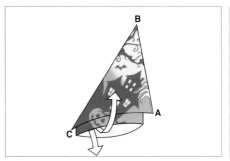

5 Open corner C, flattening the crease BC.

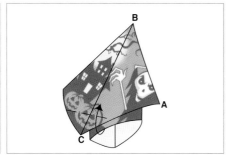

6 Fold up the tip of corner C...

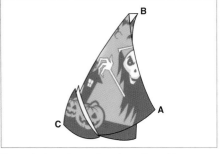

7 ...to lock and complete the sail napkin.

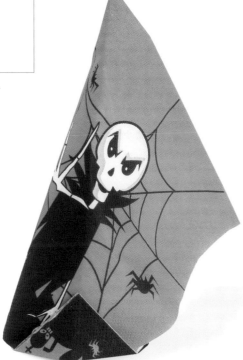

These spooky napkins came from a local grocery store, but there are thousands of designs available online.

Fan

SKILL LEVEL

You will need

❏ 18in (44cm) square paper napkin

THIS IS A SIMPLE BUT VERY ATTRACTIVE NAPKIN FOLD THAT IS EQUALLY EFFECTIVE WITH FABRIC OR PAPER NAPKINS. FOR A REALLY CRISP FOLD, USE AN IRON: WITH PAPER NAPKINS, TURN THE STEAM OFF; WITH FABRIC NAPKINS, SPRAY STARCH AND A LITTLE STEAM WILL GIVE YOU A NEAT EDGE.

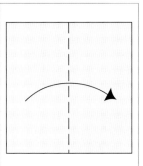

1 Fold in half and crease firmly.

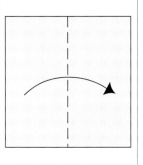

2 Pleat down the napkin every ½in (1.5cm) to just past halfway, finishing with the pleats on top.

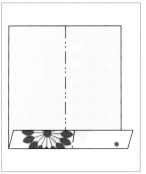

3 Mountain fold the napkin and pinch the center of the pleats firmly.

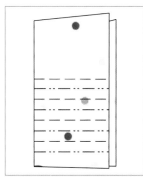

4 Open edges at the top, fold the unpleated edges down to lie along the pleats.

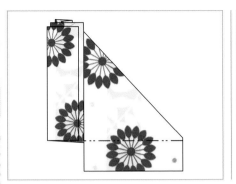

5 Fold the overhanging end underneath to hold the napkin together. Crease firmly.

6 Stand the napkin upright and spread out the pleats. Use the triangular bracket to support the fan.

When using patterned napkins, try aligning them in different ways in step 1 to find the most attractive final effect.

Flame

SKILL LEVEL

THIS FOLD IS DESIGNED FOR A WINE GLASS; BUT THE BASE COULD ALSO BE HELD IN A NAPKIN RING. FOR A REALLY DRAMATIC EFFECT, USE A NAPKIN WITH DIFFERENT COLORED SIDES, OR MORE THAN ONE CONTRASTING NAPKIN IN EACH GLASS.

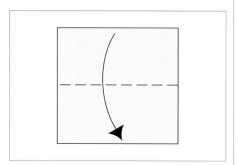

1 Fold the top edge down to the bottom.

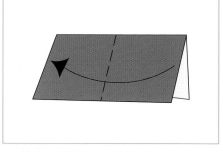

2 Fold the right-hand edge over to the left.

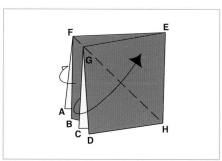

3 Fold A and B behind to touch E; fold C and D to the front to touch E. Crease FH and GH...

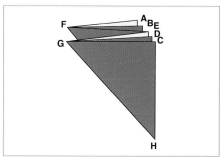

4 ...like this.

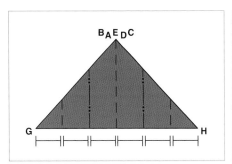

5 Pleat the triangle into six equal vertical divisions, to look...

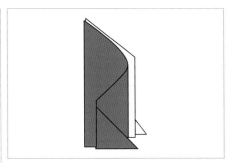

6 ...like this.

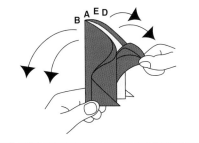

7 Hold the napkin firmly at the bottom. There are five layers of corners at the top. Tug corner C as shown, pulling it as far out as possible. Do the same with corner D next to it, but not pulling it as far. Repeat on the other side, pulling B further than A. Insert into a glass or napkin ring.

Be careful of candles on your dinner table as the corners of the napkin are just the right height to catch fire.

Cockade

SKILL LEVEL

You will need
❏ 13in (33cm) square paper napkin

THIS IS ONE OF THE MOST DECORATIVE AND SPECTACULAR NAPKIN FOLDS, IMPRESSIVE ENOUGH TO USE ON THE MOST IMPORTANT OCCASIONS. IT'S SURE TO MAKE A BIG IMPACT ON YOUR DINNER GUESTS.

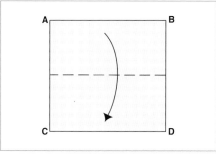

1 If the napkin is already folded into quarters (as most are), skip forward to step 3; otherwise, fold AB down to CD.

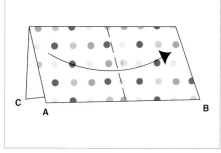

2 Fold AC across to BD.

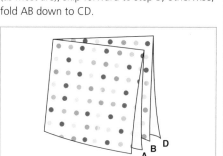

3 Note CABD. Rotate to step 4 position.

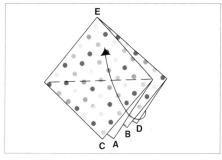

4 Fold CABD up to E.

5 Fold the sloping edges of the triangle inward so that FE and GE meet in the middle.

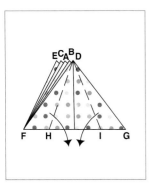

6 Fold F and G behind to form a straight edge between H and I.

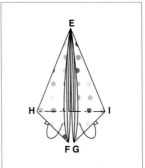

7 Fold I behind, folding the shape in half down the middle.

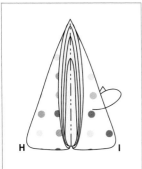

8 Grip H and I firmly with one hand. With the other hand, pull D out as far as possible from the nest of layers. Pull out B, but not as far as D, then A, and finally C.

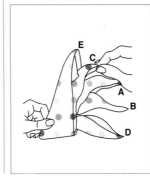

9 The finished napkin.

To create double-sided napkins, choose matching paper napkins and peel the top two tissue sheets from each. Iron them together without steam.

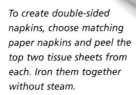

Swan

See also
Kite base, page 20

SKILL LEVEL

You will need

❏ Fabric napkin
❏ Smaller square of aluminum foil

THIS IS MORE OF A CENTERPIECE THAN A CONVENTIONAL NAPKIN FOLD, BUT IT IS FUN, AND MORE CHALLENGING. LAY THE FOIL ON TOP OF THE NAPKIN BEFORE YOU FOLD THE KITE BASE—THIS WILL GIVE THE SWAN ENOUGH STIFFNESS TO STAND UPRIGHT.

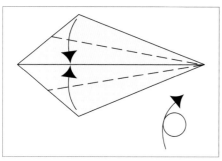

1 Begin with the kite base face down. Fold long edges to the center crease. Turn over.

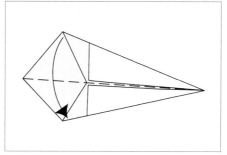

2 Valley fold along the center crease.

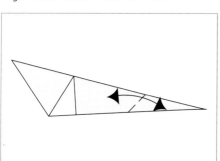

3 Fold the point back to create the neck; crease firmly. Unfold.

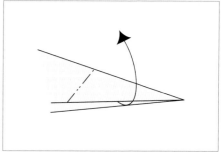

4 Make an outside reverse fold using the creases made in step 3.

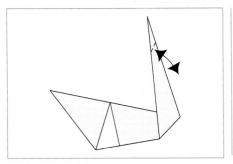

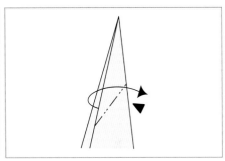

5 Fold the tip of the point forward to form a beak; crease firmly. Unfold.

6 Make an outside reverse fold using the creases made in step 5.

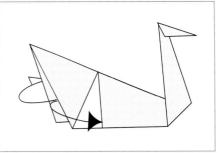

7 Open the bottom folds slightly to create a base for the swan.

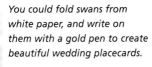

You could fold swans from white paper, and write on them with a gold pen to create beautiful wedding placecards.

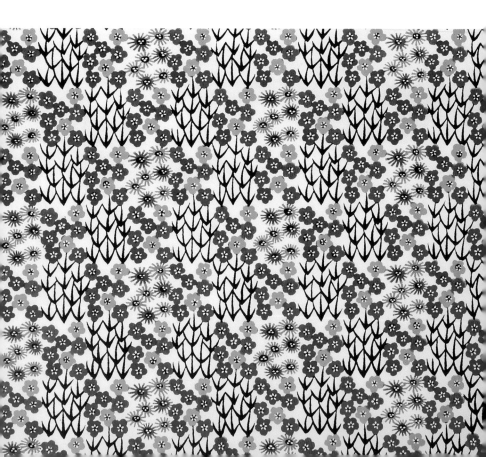

ANIMALS AND FLOWERS

There are thousands of designs for origami animals and flowers—some are very simple, others are huge and elaborate. They are extremely popular among folders of all abilities; this is possibly because the models are not judged by abstract aesthetic rules but by a single phrase; "can you guess what it is yet?" Fold a cat or a frog in a crowded room, and you will soon be the focus of a large and interested audience!

See also
Preliminary base,
page 21

Crane

SKILL LEVEL

You will need

❏ 6in (15cm) square of light- or
medium-weight paper in a
preliminary base

THE CRANE IS PROBABLY THE BEST-
KNOWN ORIGAMI DESIGN DUE TO THE
POPULARITY OF THE STORY OF SADAKO
SASAKI (SEE PAGE 7) AND THE ADOPTION
OF THE DESIGN AS THE SYMBOL OF THE
WORLD PEACE MOVEMENT.

1 With the
open end
of the base
pointing
downward,
fold both sides
in to meet the
center crease,
then unfold.

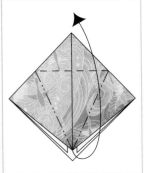

2 Fold down
the top corner
as shown.
Unfold. Lift
the top flap
at the bottom
end and fold
it upward,
allowing the
sides to come
inward. This is
a petal fold.

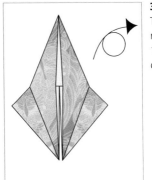

3 Crease flat.
Turn over and
repeat steps
1–3 on the
other side.

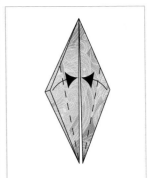

4 With the
open end
pointing
downward,
fold both sides
in to meet the
center crease.
Repeat on the
other side.

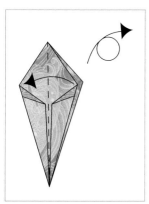

5 Fold one layer over to the left, then turn the model over.

6 Repeat step 5 on this side. The model should now be symmetrical.

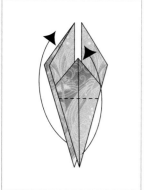

7 Fold the bottom point up to meet the top points. Repeat on the other side.

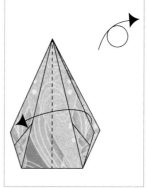

8 Fold one layer over to the left, turn the model over, and repeat. The model should now be symmetrical.

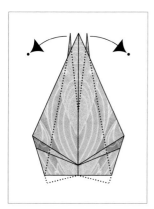

9 Fold the inner points outward to the positions indicated.

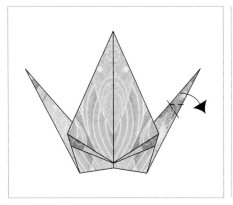

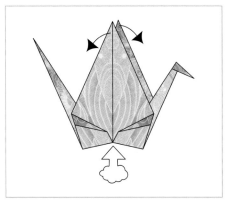

10 Reverse-fold to create the head.

11 Pull the wings apart gently and blow into the hole in the bottom to inflate.

To create cranes on strings, like the Senbarazu on page 7, use a darning needle to thread string through the cranes, and add a bead to the end of the string.

Butterfly

SKILL LEVEL

AKIRA YOSHIZAWA WAS THE FATHER OF MODERN ORIGAMI. THIS IS HIS BEST-KNOWN BUTTERFLY, THE LOGO OF THE INTERNATIONAL ORIGAMI CENTER, FOUNDED TO HELP SPREAD FRIENDSHIP AND PEACE THROUGH THE ORIGAMI WORLD. IT IS SHOWN HERE WITHOUT WRITTEN INSTRUCTIONS, AS HE ORIGINALLY INTENDED.

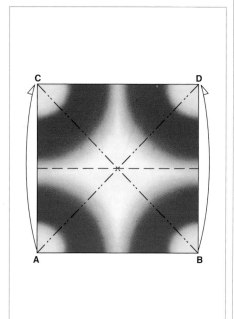

1

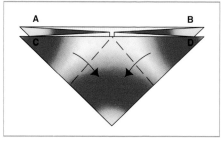

2

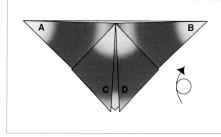

3

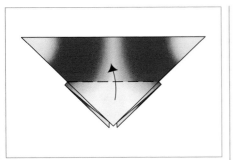

4

5

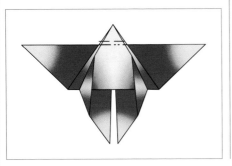

6

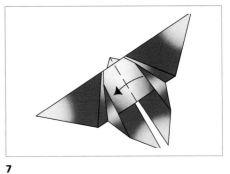

7

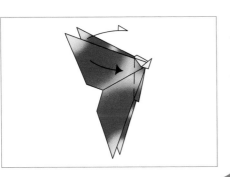

8

Try hanging your origami butterflies from the ceiling using thread, or attach one to a handmade card.

Fox

SKILL LEVEL

You will need

❏ 6in x 3in (15cm x 7.5cm) of light- or
   medium-weight paper

**Artist's tip: To make baby animals, use
light-weight paper that is half the size of
the parent model. Check proportions
before cutting multiple squares. Tweezers
are handy for little noses and ears!**

THE STYLIZATION TYPICAL OF JAPANESE
DESIGNS IS SHOWN TO GOOD EFFECT
IN THIS DESIGN BY MITSUE OKUDA.
WHAT'S MORE, ALTHOUGH IT IS NOT
SYMMETRICAL, THE DESIGN LOOKS
GOOD FROM ALL ANGLES. THE MOST
EFFECTIVE ORIGAMI IS ALSO OFTEN
THE SIMPLEST!

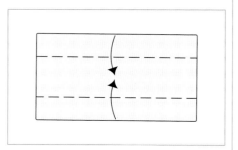

1 Fold the long edges to the center crease.

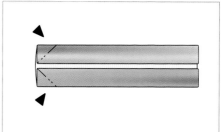

2 Reverse twice on the left.

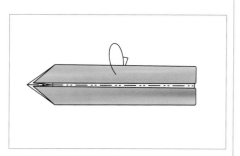

3 Mountain fold in half.

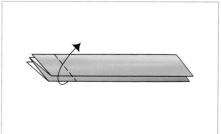

4 Valley fold.

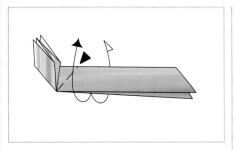

5 Outside-reverse.

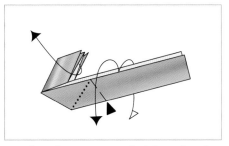

6 Pull two layers across to the left to allow the center point (the nose) to rise. Outside-reverse on the right, as shown.

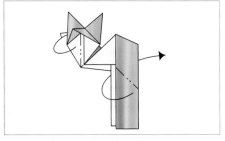

7 Mountain the tail. Fold the left ear around the back.

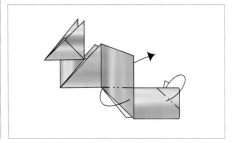

8 Narrow the tip of the tail. Mountain fold the tail behind.

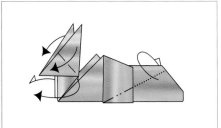

9 Narrow the tail. Pull the ears forward.

When you're making families of animals, use the same pattern or type of paper so that their relationship is clear.

Cat

See also
Kite base, page 20

SKILL LEVEL

You will need

❏ 6in (15cm) square of light- or medium-weight paper for kite base

Artist's tip: Choose your paper design carefully to suggest the coloring and markings of your origami animal. The pattern in this paper design gives a lovely tortoiseshell effect.

THE CAT IS A TRICKY SUBJECT TO CAPTURE IN PAPER BECAUSE OF ITS CURVED AND FLUID FORM. ORIGAMI EXPERTS WOULD AGREE THAT TOSHIE TAKAHAMA'S DESIGN IS THE MOST SUCCESSFUL YET. AS YOU WILL SEE, IT IS CHARACTERFUL AND INSTANTLY RECOGNIZABLE.

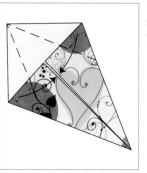

1 Fold the short edges to the center.

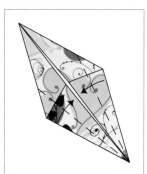

2 Narrow the corner at the right. Keep the corner as neat as possible. Repeat on the left.

3 Fold in half. Note A and B.

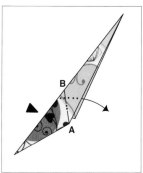

4 Reverse the blunt corner along AB, then...

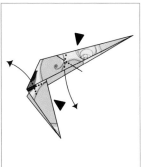

5 ...reverse it back up level with the open edge. Reverse the sharp corner to the position shown in step 6.

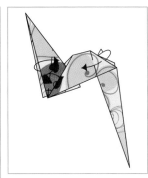

6 Valley the front layer at the left across to the right, so that the point stands upright. Turn the sharp point inside out as shown.

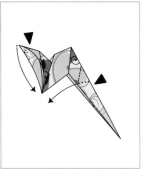

7 Squash the point. Reverse the tail.

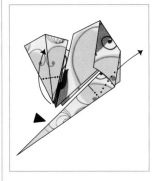

8 Tuck the point inside the face, folding as shown. Reverse the tail.

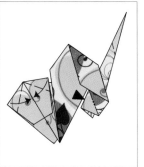

9 Fold the ears forward. Reverse the hind legs. Outside-reverse the tail.

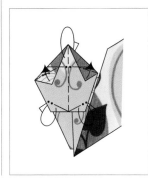

10 Shape the nose. Fold the top of the head behind. Fold up the ears.

See also
Preliminary base,
page 21
Kite base, page 20

Tulip

SKILL LEVEL

THE TULIP IS ONE OF THE SIMPLEST AND
MOST APPEALING OF ALL ORIGAMI
FLOWERS. ITS JAPANESE CREATOR,
KUNIHIKO KASAHARA, HAS WRITTEN
OVER 100 ORIGAMI BOOKS—INCLUDING
SOME IN ENGLISH—THAT FEATURE HIS
OWN PROLIFIC OUTPUT.

Petals

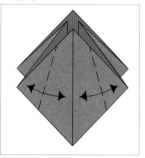

1 Begin with
the preliminary
base. With the
open corner
at the top,
fold the front
corners to the
center crease.
Repeat behind.

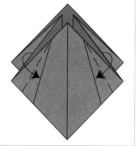

2 Fold the
open edges
to the crease.
Repeat behind.

3 Fold over
along step 1
creases. Repeat
behind.

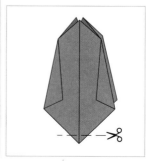

4 With a pair
of scissors,
snip off the tip.
Snip off less
than you think
you should—
the hole can
be enlarged,
but cannot be
made smaller!

5 Gently open out the flower, rounding out the sides as you go.

Stem

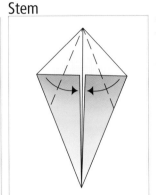

6 Begin with the kite base. Fold the short edges to the center crease.

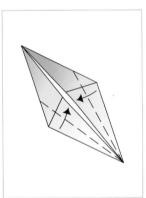

7 Fold the long sides to the center to narrow.

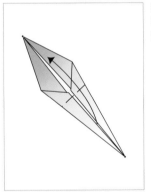

8 Fold in half, points together.

9 Pull the sharp point out to the dotted position. Squeeze the paper flat at the bottom to let the sharp point retain its new position.

10 The stem is complete. Insert the sharp spike into the base of the petals.

Frog

SKILL LEVEL

THIS TAKE ON A TRADITIONAL JUMPING FROG IS A HUGE FAVORITE WITH ALL CHILDREN, AND, WITH SOME HELP, IT IS REASONABLY EASY FOR THEM TO CREATE A SIMPLIFIED VERSION WITH ALL SORTS OF EXCITING PAPERS.

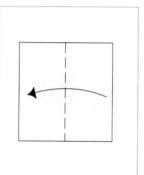

1 Starting with the white side of the paper upward, fold the square in half down the middle.

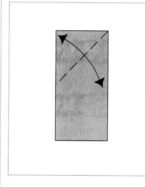

2 Fold the left-hand corner down to meet the opposite edge. Unfold.

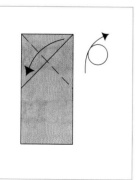

3 Repeat on the right-hand side. Turn the paper over.

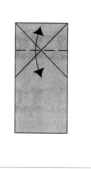

4 Valley fold the top of the paper so the crease bisects the previous creases. Then unfold.

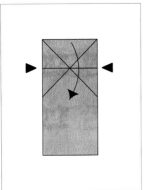

5 Use existing creases to create two squash folds, one on either side. Turn over.

6 Valley fold the nose of the frog, and then sink it inside the head. (Leave this step out for young children.) Fold the bottom of the paper up to lie along the bottom of the triangle.

7 Fold the sides into the middle and crease firmly.

8 Fold the bottom of the paper in half again, crease firmly, and unfold.

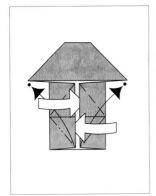

9 Take hold of the inside corners at the bottom, and pull the corners out and up. Flatten the paper so that two triangles are formed inside the layers. Crease firmly.

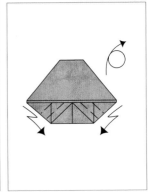

10 Pleat as shown to form the back legs. Turn over.

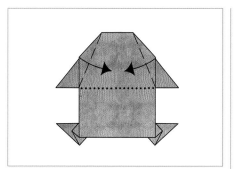

11 Fold in the two front corners to create pop-up eyes.

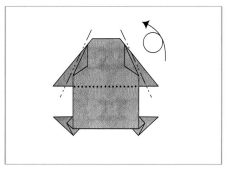

12 Fold the front legs underneath so that they are hidden by the frog's body again. Turn over.

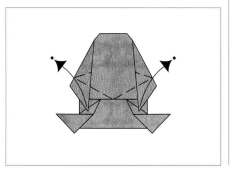

13 Pull the frog's legs out to the points shown, and crease flat.

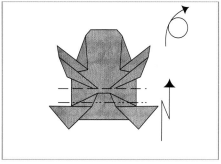

14 Pleat the back legs as shown, pressing the creases very hard to create the spring. Turn over and start hopping!

To make your frog jump, press down on the back end, compressing the pleat, and let your finger slide off.

Rooster

SKILL LEVEL ▲▲▲

THIS DESIGN, BY FLORENCE TEMKO OF THE USA, IS A FANTASTIC EXAMPLE OF ORIGAMI THAT IS INSTANTLY RECOGNIZABLE WHILE STILL LOOKING FOLDED—WHICH, CURIOUSLY, NOT ALL ORIGAMI DOES.

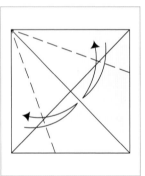

1 Fold the left and top edges to the center crease. Unfold.

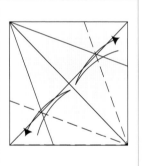

2 Repeat for the right and bottom edges.

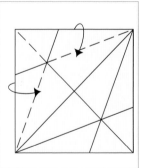

3 Fold in the three creases as shown, so that the top corner stands upright...

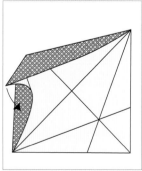

4 ...like this. Flatten it to the left.

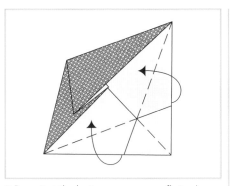

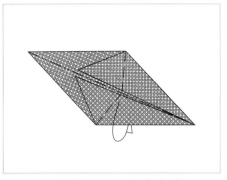

5 Repeat at the bottom, once more flattening the loose corner to the left.

6 Mountain the bottom portion behind the top.

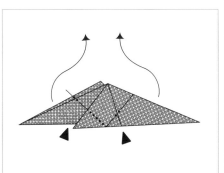

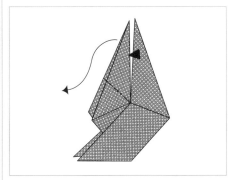

7 Reverse twice.

8 Reverse.

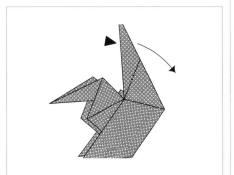

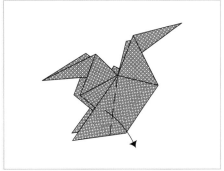

9 Reverse. Note the angle.

10 Valley; repeat behind.

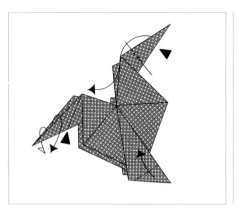

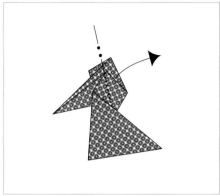

11 At the left, outside-reverse. At the right, reverse. Valley the feet. Repeat behind. The valley creases on the feet should be at such an angle that the rooster can balance.

12 Reverse the beak.

These roosters are made with authentic Japanese papers that enhance the traditional look of the design.

Rabbit

See also
Waterbomb base,
page 22

SKILL LEVEL

You will need

- ❏ 6in (15cm) square light- or medium-weight paper (waterbomb base)
- ❏ 9in (22cm) square light- or medium-weight paper (waterbomb base)

THERE ARE MANY ORIGAMI BUNNIES FOR YOU TO TRY, BUT HERE IS ONE WITH A DIFFERENCE: IT IS ONE OF THE FEW MADE FROM TWO PIECES, AND THE ONLY ONE IN WHICH BOTH SECTIONS OF THE DESIGN ARE BLOW-UPS.

BODY

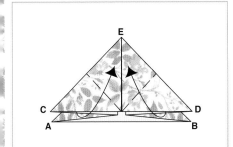

1 Using the 9in (22cm) waterbomb base, fold C and D up to E.

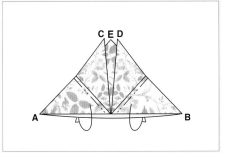

2 Fold A and B behind to E.

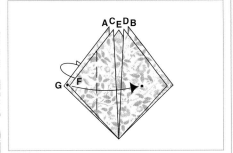

3 Fold F across to the right so that it goes a little beyond the crease shown. Repeat behind with G.

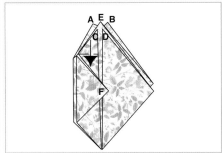

4 Fold down corner C. Repeat behind with A.

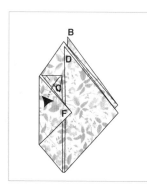

5 Valley-fold the small triangle as shown, and tuck it between the two layers of paper that run down to F. Repeat behind with A.

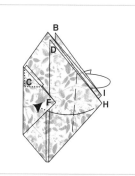

6 Fold H across to the left, tucking it underneath F. Repeat behind with I.

HEAD

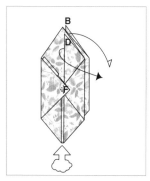

7 Fold down D along the edge that runs down to H. Repeat with B behind. Carefully blow into the hole at the bottom to inflate the body.

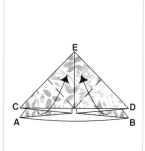

8 Using the 6in (15cm) base, fold C and D up to E.

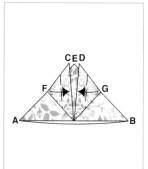

9 Fold F and G into the middle.

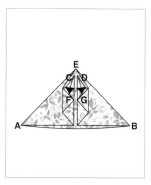

10 Fold down C and D.

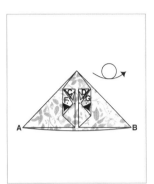

11 As in step 5 of the body, valley-fold the small triangles just formed where shown, and tuck them between the two layers of paper that run to F and G. Turn over.

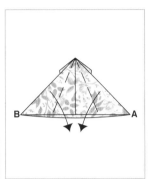

12 Fold down B and A as shown.

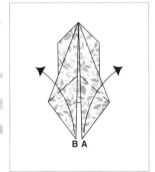

13 Fold B and A back out at such an angle that BA forms a long horizontal edge.

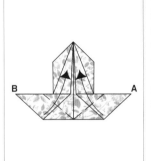

14 Fold up B and A as shown, so that the bottom edge lies along the middle crease. These are the ears.

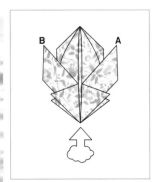

15 As for the body, carefully blow into the hole at the bottom to inflate the head. Then use a little paper glue to attach the head to the top of the body.

Alter the angle of the head and ears, or add extra folds, to change the rabbit's expression.

Tortoise

SKILL LEVEL

You will need

☐ 12in (30cm) square of thin green paper

Artist's tip: Keep track of which end is which from step 20, or you'll end up with a tortoise with a flat head!

THIS IS A TRICKY DESIGN BUT WELL WORTH PERFECTING, IF ONLY BECAUSE OF THE LOVELY DOMED SHELL AND WRINKLED FACE.

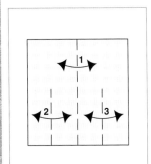

1 Begin with the white side up. Fold the paper in half vertically and unfold. Then fold the sides into the center line, crease the lower part, and unfold.

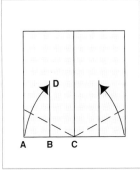

2 Fold corner A up to lie on line BD. Note that the crease hits the bottom edge of the paper at point C, the middle of the bottom edge. Repeat on the right side.

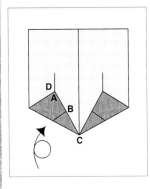

3 Turn the paper over.

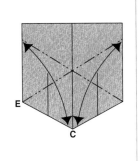

4 Fold corner C up to lie along the left edge—the crease runs through point E. Unfold. Repeat on the right.

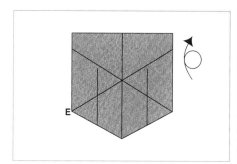

5 Turn over the paper.

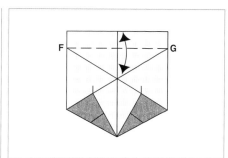

6 Fold down the top edge along a crease running between points F and G (where the two diagonal creases hit the edges). Unfold.

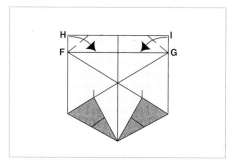

7 Fold down corner H to lie on line FG; the crease hits the edge at point F. Repeat for corner I.

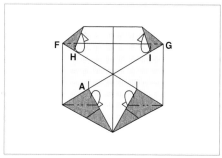

8 Fold corners A and H underneath. Repeat on the right. (This is easily done by unfolding flap A, making the fold, and refolding.)

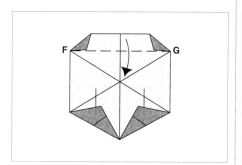

9 Fold the top edge down along the existing crease FG.

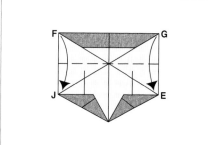

10 Fold down corners F and G to meet corners J and E, respectively.

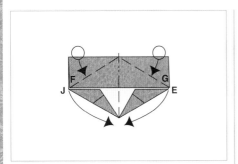

11 Bring corners J, F, G, and E together at the bottom of the model (it will not lie flat).

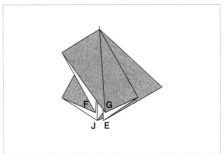

12 Flatten the paper out. Note that the top flap swings to the left and the rear flap swings to the right.

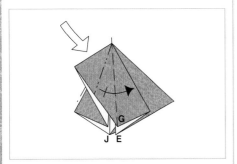

13 Squash-fold the top flap.

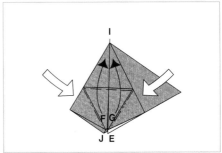

14 Squash-fold each side. Fold corners F and G up to point I.

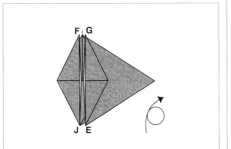

15 Turn the model over from side to side.

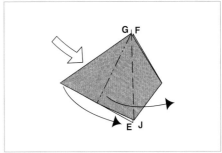

16 Squash-fold the large point.

17 Reverse-fold the side corners.

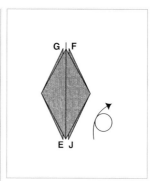

18 Turn the model over from side to side.

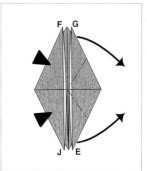

19 Reverse-fold two points to the right.

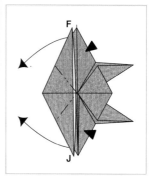

20 Repeat on the left.

21 Reverse-fold all four points.

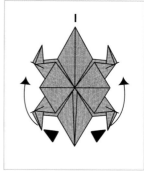

22 Reverse-fold the bottom pair of points upward. Be sure that point I (the thick point) is at the top.

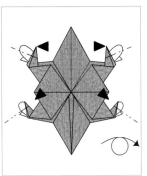

23 Reverse-fold the tips of all four points. Turn the model over.

24 Fold the bottom point (the tail) in thirds and unfold. You don't need to make the creases run all the way up.

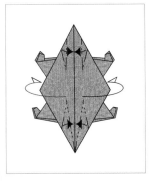

25 Curve the sides of the body away from you; at the same time, crimp the top and bottom of the model. The shell will bulge upward in the middle.

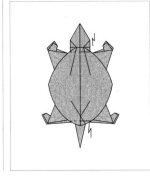

26 Pleat neck and tail to lock. Puff up the head slightly by pulling out the middle layer. Fold the feet down. Pinch the tail in half. Round the shell.

Use different-sized papers to make a family of tortoises— this design is trickier the smaller it gets, so you will need lighter-weight paper if you want to take up the challenge.

Daffodil

See also
Hexagon, page 24
Flapping bird,
page 134

SKILL LEVEL

You will need

☐ 8in (20cm) hexagon of fine-textured yellow paper

☐ 8in (20cm) square of medium-weight green paper folded to step 6 of the flapping bird (see page 134)

TECHNICALLY, THIS DESIGN BY TED NORMINTON OF THE UK IS THE MOST ADVANCED IN THIS CHAPTER AND SHOULD ONLY BE ATTEMPTED BY EXPERIENCED FOLDERS. HOWEVER, EVEN IF YOU ARE UNABLE TO ACHIEVE THIS STRAIGHTAWAY, IT IS GREAT PRACTICE TO TRY TO CONSTRUCT SUCH A COMPLEX DESIGN.

PETALS

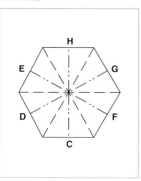

1 Crease mountains and valleys in the yellow hexagon as shown, collapsing them to make the shape shown in step 2.

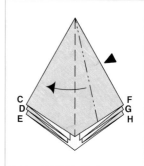

2 If the bottom edge runs straight across, turn the whole shape inside out to make the shape seen here. Lift F and squash...

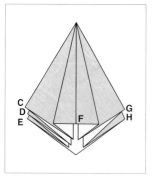

3 ...like this. Repeat with C, D, E, G, and H. When squashing, try to keep the same number of layers left and right.

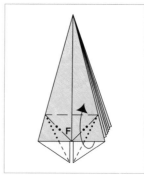

4 Lift point F along the marked creases (petal fold).

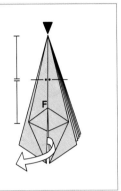

5 Unfold the step 4 creases. Repeat five more times. Invert the top corner down into the body of the paper, at the level shown. To do this, open out the hexagon, then collapse it back into shape when you have creased the rim of the sink into a continuous mountain fold and when you have inverted the center.

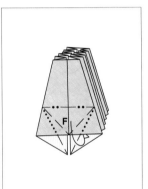

6 Tuck F up inside the front layer, reversing some of the step 4 creases. Repeat five more times around the layers.

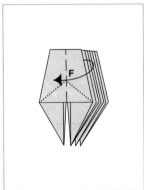

7 Fold one layer across to the left, to reveal...

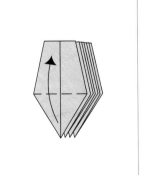

8 ...a clean face. Fold up the bottom triangle. Repeat five more times around the layers.

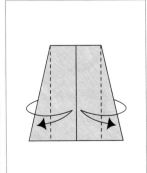

9 Note that for clarity, only the front layer will now be shown. Crease and unfold as shown.

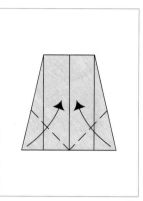

10 Fold the corners up to the center crease.

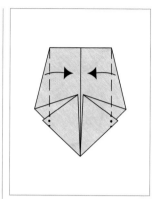

11 Re-fold the step 10 creases, so that the bottom portion of each crease disappears into the lower triangle.

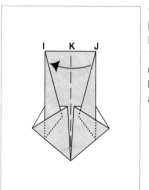

12 Fold the layer across. Repeat steps 10–12 five more times. Note I, J, and K.

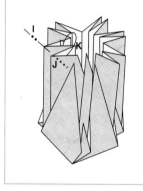

13 Fold K behind, forming a small triangle, so that I and J are brought together and locked. Repeat five more times within the trumpet.

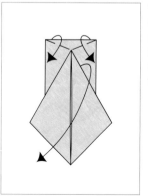

14 Pull down each of the six petals and reverse the rim of the trumpet to shape it.

The intricate details in the bloom folds can be difficult to reproduce, so fold slowly and carefully.

STEM

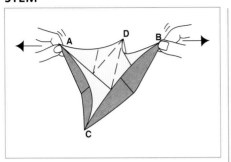

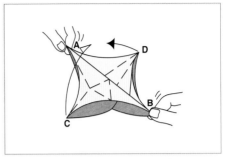

15 Hold the flapping bird as shown. Pull A and B smartly apart, until the diagonal that connects them pops into a rigid mountain crease…

16 …like this. Flatten, bringing C and D together.

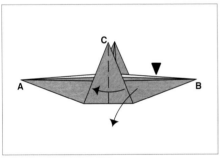

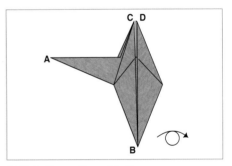

17 Fold the triangle in half below C, swiveling B downward.

18 Note the position of B. Turn over.

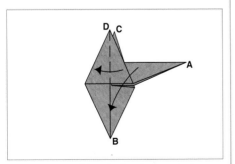

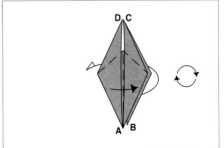

19 Repeat step 17, swiveling A down to B.

20 Fold a layer across at the front. Repeat behind but on the opposite side. Rotate the paper 180 degrees.

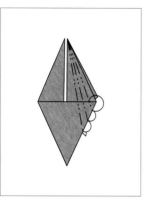

21 Narrow the front layer at the right. Repeat behind. Fold the middle crease first.

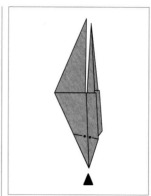

22 Push in or sink the bottom corner. Note that the crease tilts upward at the left. Repeat behind.

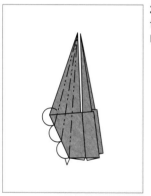

23 Narrow the flap on the left. Repeat behind.

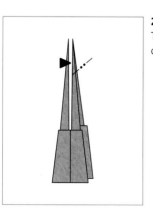

24 Reverse. The stem is complete.

Insert the top spike into the back of the petals to create the finished daffodil.

Corgi

SKILL LEVEL

THIS DESIGN BY GUSPATH GO FROM HONG KONG LOOKS DECEPTIVELY SIMPLE. THE FIRST NINE STEPS ARE PRE-FOLDING AND NEED TO BE VERY PRECISE. STEPS 15 AND 22 ARE TRICKY—MAKE SURE YOU LOOK AHEAD TO THE NEXT DIAGRAMS BEFORE FOLDING.

You will need

☐ 12in (30cm) square of cardstock

Artist's tip: Choose your paper color carefully. Using tan and white paper gives a classic Corgi look—if you use reddish-brown it will look like a fox!

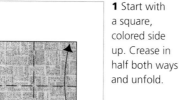

1 Start with a square, colored side up. Crease in half both ways and unfold.

2 Fold the lower left quarter section in half both ways, then unfold.

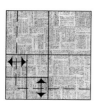

3 Add creases on the lower and left sides, creasing only where indicated.

4 Fold the center point of the lower edge to meet the vertical crease indicated. Crease and unfold. Repeat with the center point of the left edge.

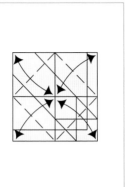

5 Turn over and fold all four corners to the center, crease, and unfold.

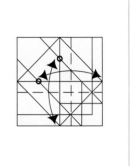

6 Fold the center points of the lower and right edges to meet the circled crease intersections.

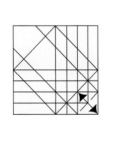

7 Fold the lower right corner to the nearest crease intersection, crease, and unfold.

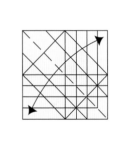

8 Fold the lower left to upper right corner, crease a diagonal, then unfold.

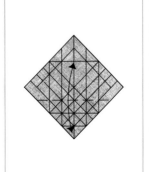

9 Turn back to the colored side and rotate the paper to this position. Fold the lower corner to the upper crease intersection, crease, and unfold.

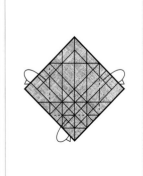

10 Refold underneath three of the creases made in step 5.

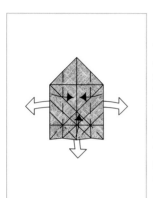

11 Fold the lower edge to the original center. At the same time, fold the left and right sides to the center, allowing the flaps to pop out from underneath.

12 This is the result. Mountain fold in half.

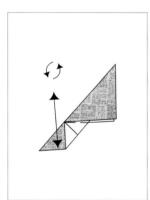

13 Rotate the paper to this position. Fold the lower section upward along the raw edge, crease, then unfold.

14 Crease the lower section in half, then partially unfold the paper underneath.

15 Change the creases indicated so they match this pattern of valleys and mountains. The paper will collapse flat again, if you are careful.

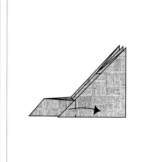

16 Fold the small triangular flap to the right. Repeat on the other side.

17 Make an outside reverse fold on the tip of the tail.

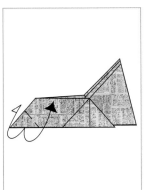

18 Fold the tail to meet the vertical crease. Crease and unfold.

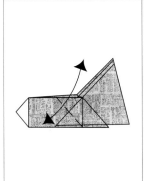

19 Fold the tail in half, creasing as far as the previous crease.

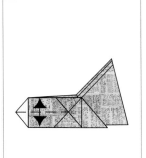

20 Open the top of the tail slightly to make these creases. See the next step, showing the move from above and behind, halfway through.

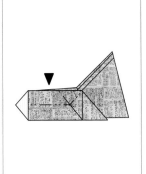

21 Sink the point at the tip of the tail by applying pressure so that it is "popped" inside. This is known as a closed sink, which locks the point inside the sink.

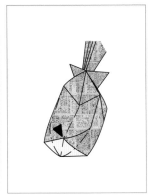

22 Flatten the tail again using these creases— hold the tail in one hand, the back legs in the other, and gently press them together.

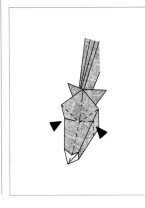

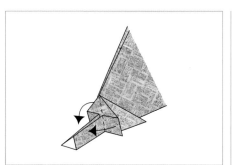

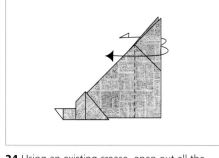

23 This is the result. Fold the loose flaps backward.

24 Using an existing crease, open out all the layers, allowing the head to fold forward naturally.

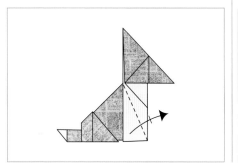

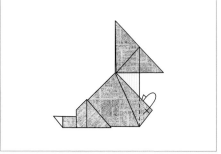

25 Fold the first layer forward on a crease between the back of the head and the lower right corner. Repeat on the other side.

26 Tuck the excess paper inside the model, front, and back.

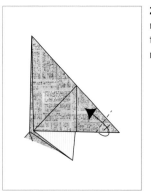

27 Outside reverse-fold the tip of the nose.

A pair of alert little Corgis.

See also
Preliminary base,
page 21

Vase of flowers

SKILL LEVEL

You will need

- ❑ 6in (15cm) square (preliminary base)
- ❑ Letter (A4) medium-weight green paper
- ❑ 12in (30cm) square of textured cardstock
- ❑ Paper glue
- ❑ Green floral tape
- ❑ Florist's wires
- ❑ Scissors
- ❑ Rice grains

Artist's tip: Using specialist origami flower paper means that your iris will have a colored center and variegated petals.

THIS PROJECT WILL REQUIRE THE MOST TIME AND THE MOST EQUIPMENT, AND WILL ALSO TAKE THE MOST ARTISTRY TO DESIGN AND ARRANGE. HOWEVER, IT IS DECEPTIVELY SIMPLE TO FOLD AND IT MAKES A STUNNING CENTERPIECE FOR ANY OCCASION.

IRIS

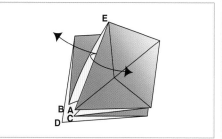

1 Start with a preliminary base. Lift E so that it stands vertically. Press the folded edge to open the pocket inside E. Hold ABCD neatly together.

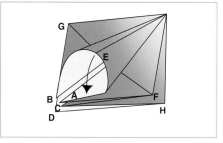

2 Continue to press on E, until it squashes flat. Crease it firmly.

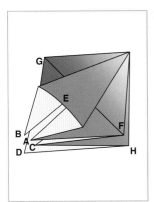

3 Turn over.

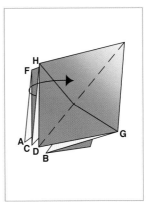

4 Lift up H...

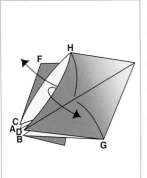

5 ...and press down on the fold to open its pocket, as in step 2. Squash H flat. Keep the points ABCD together.

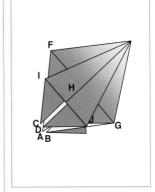

6 It should look like this. Fold I over to touch J. Then lift F so that it stands upright. Press down on the fold to squash it flat. Turn over and repeat with G.

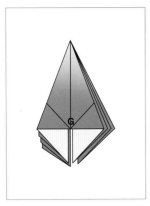

7 All four flaps are now squashed and the paper is symmetrical.

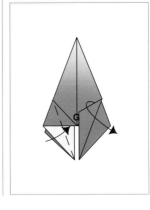

8 Fold in the side points of the top layer at the lower, broader end to lie along the central crease, G. The right-hand side is shown folded. Unfold.

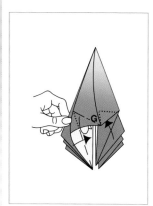

9 With one hand, lift up G. With the other, re-form the creases made in step 8. Push these folds under G, using the mountain creases from the base, until the paper lies flat.

10 Turn over.

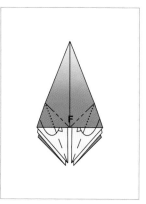

11 Repeat steps 8–10 on either side of F, E, and H.

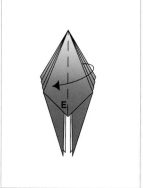

12 The paper is now completely symmetrical, with four layers on each side. Fold one layer from the right over to the left.

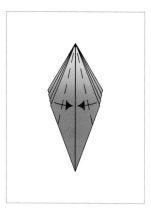

13 This will expose a blank face. Fold in the top edges of the upper layer so they lie along the middle. Keep it neat!

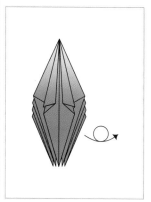

14 This is the result. Turn over.

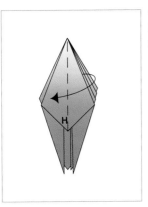

15 Fold one layer over from right to left.

16 Fold as in step 13. Repeat the process for the other two blank faces. The paper will crease more easily and neatly if the layers are symmetrical.

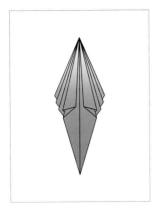

17 It should now look like this. Move the layers around so that there are four either side of the center, but so that the top layer is the one you have just folded. Turn upside down.

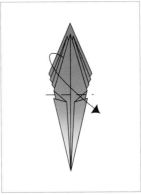

18 The iris now has a narrow stem. Fold down the petal facing you...

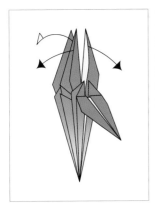

19 ...like this. Turn over, and fold down the opposite petal. Repeat with the other two petals...

20 ...like this. Now loosely roll each of the petals in turn, around a pencil. This will give them a soft, curled shape.

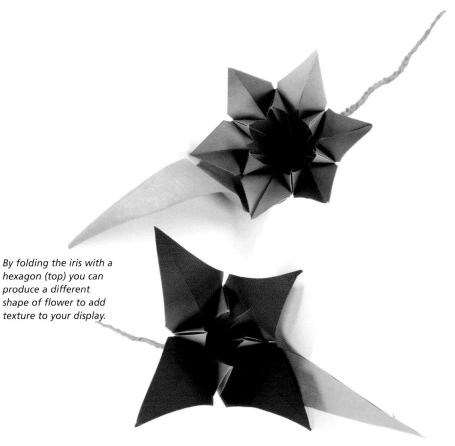

By folding the iris with a hexagon (top) you can produce a different shape of flower to add texture to your display.

LEAVES AND WIRING

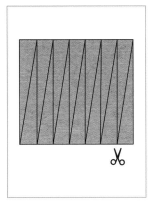

21 Cut the green paper sheet into long tapering strips, as shown. One sheet will make 12 or more leaves.

22 Fold the paper in half at the square end by about 1in (2cm). Curl the tip of the leaf. With a pair of scissors, cut out a small V-shape in the middle of the crease, not too near the end.

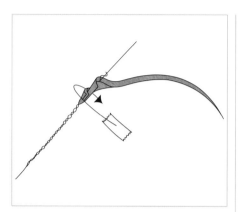

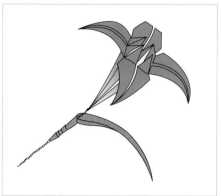

23 Overlap two florist's wires and twist them together. For longer stems, simply twist in more wires. Poke one end of the wire through the cut in the leaf, position the leaf a little way down the wire, and then twist the square end of the leaf tight around the wire, at such an angle that the leaf points upward, not horizontally. Secure the end of the twisted leaf with a piece of sticky tape.

24 Push the end of the wire through the bottom of the iris by moistening the paper with your tongue. Once through, bend over the top of the wire, and then drop the end back into the flower until it catches tight near the base of the stem. Wind green tape onto the wire, starting at the bottom. At the top, wind the tape around the base of the iris, pulling it tight to secure the iris to the wire. Wind the tape to the bottom of the stem.

Using green floral tape to wrap the wires and attach the flowers makes the stems less noticeable.

VASE

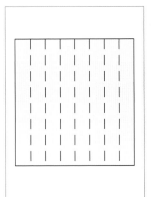

25 Divide the cardstock square into eighths, using valley folds.

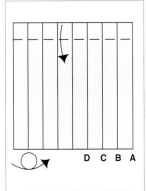

26 Fold down the top edge by about 1in (2cm). Turn over.

D C B A

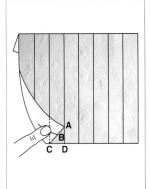

27 Fold A across to touch crease D. Make a sloping crease between lines B and C that will exactly touch C. Make sure this crease does not extend beyond C.

A
B
C D

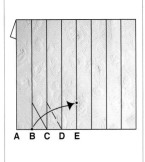

28 Unfold, moving A back to its original position. The crease should be to the left of C. Repeat step 27, this time folding B over to E to make a crease between C and D.

A B C D E

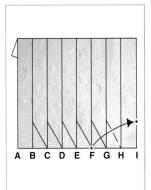

29 Keep repeating this move by folding C to crease F, then D to crease G, E to crease H, and F to the right-hand edge (I). The creases should look like this.

A B C D E F G H I

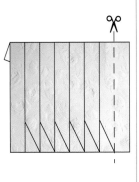

30 Fold a crease that runs into B, from the left-hand edge, parallel to the crease that runs into C. Cut off the right-hand eighth of paper. Turn over.

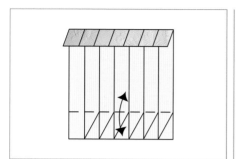

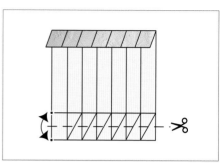

31 Make a horizontal valley crease that connects the tops of all the sloping creases. Unfold.

32 Fold the bottom edge up to the horizontal crease just made. Then cut along this crease, discarding the bottom piece.

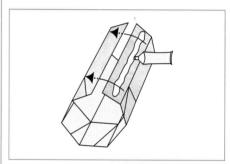

Before arranging the flowers, weight the vase with tapioca balls or rice. This helps the iris stems to stand up straight, instead of falling to the edges of the vase.

33 Reinforce the vertical creases to form a tube. Glue the right-hand panel, bring over the left-hand edge, and tuck the panel under it.

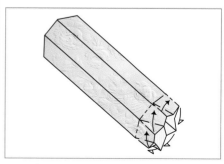

34 Push the end of the vase in so the sloping creases overlap, collapsing into the center. Glue beneath the triangles to lock them in place.

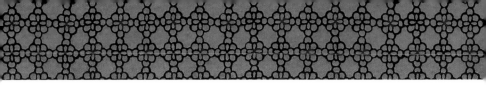

CHILDREN'S ORIGAMI

Children tend to enjoy origami—it requires no innate talent and the range of projects available is huge. It's a useful pastime on long journeys, as it requires very little in the way of preparation and materials and is relatively quiet and non-messy. All the projects in this section were picked for their amusement value— they're all toys of one kind or another, and all but two are for beginner and intermediate folders. You might need to help children follow the instructions.

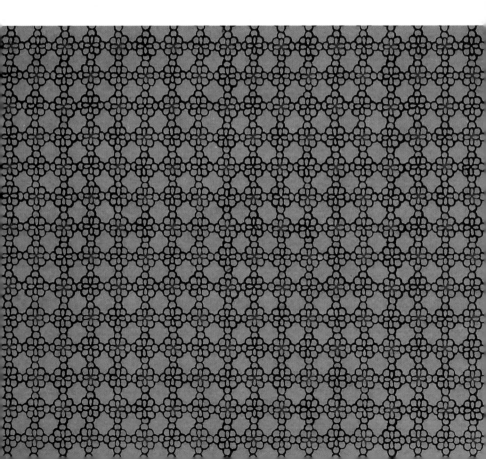

Elephant plane

SKILL LEVEL

You will need

☐ 10in (25cm) square of light- or medium-weight paper

THIS ELEPHANT ADAPTED FROM WORK BY FRENCH ARTIST ALAIN GEORGEOT HAS PARTICULARLY LARGE EARS! THIS IS A FUN DESIGN THAT FLIES AMAZINGLY WELL AND IS ENJOYABLE TO FOLD.

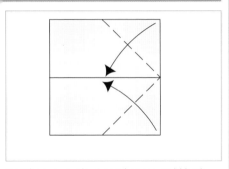

1 Make a center horizontal crease. Fold both right-hand corners to the center crease.

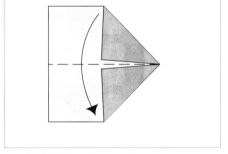

2 Valley fold from the top edge.

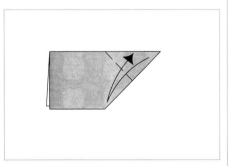

3 Fold the upper right corner to the lower right corner and unfold.

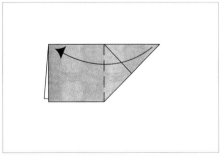

4 Fold the top right corner to the top left.

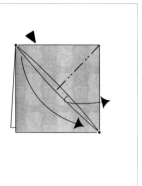

5 Using the established creases, carefully squash the loose corner flat...

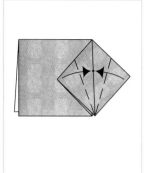

6 ...to this position. Fold both lower sides of the squashed section to the vertical center crease.

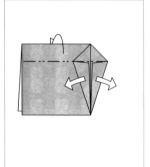

7 Mountain fold the top edge behind, along the line formed by the horizontal inside edges of the kite shape. Open the flaps back out.

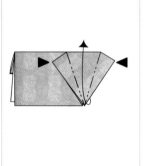

8 Fold the loose corner upward, gently pressing the sides in...

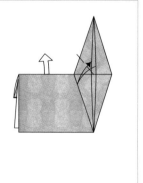

9 ...to this position. Pre-crease a small 45-degree fold on the diamond shape, then raise the hidden flap from behind.

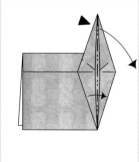

10 Add another 45-degree crease to match the last one, then use the creases shown to swing the paper across...

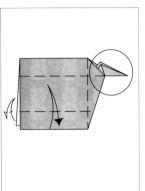

11 ...into this position. Pre-crease two shaping folds on the raw edges. The circled area is enlarged in the next three diagrams.

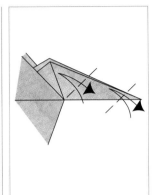

12 Make two pre-creases at about 45 degrees.

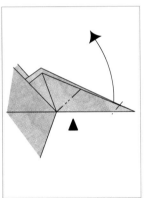

13 Use the larger to make an inside reverse fold.

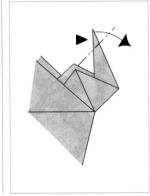

14 Then repeat with the smaller crease to shape the end of the elephant's trunk.

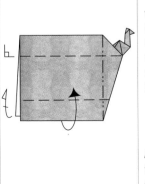

15 Fold the wings to right angles and adjust the wing tips to match the profile shown.

Like a real elephant, you'll have a hard time making her fly anywhere she doesn't want to go! Launch upward...

Banger

SKILL LEVEL

You will need

☐ 10in x 15in (25cm x 37cm) sheet of light- or medium-weight paper

Artist's tip: Larger sheets will produce louder noises.

THIS IS ONE OF THE MOST ENTERTAINING OF ALL PAPER FOLDS AND CERTAINLY THE LOUDEST! DEVOTE SOME TIME TO PRACTICING STEP 7—GOOD EXECUTION OF THE TECHNIQUE DESCRIBED WILL INCREASE THE VOLUME OF THE BANG.

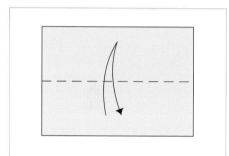

1 Fold one long edge across to the other. Crease and unfold.

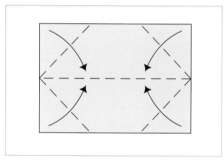

2 Fold in the corners to the center crease.

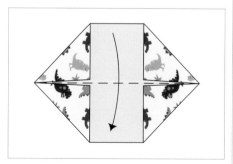

3 Fold in half along the step 1 crease.

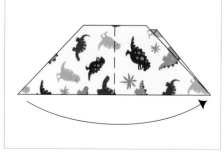

4 Mountain fold across the middle. Crease and unfold.

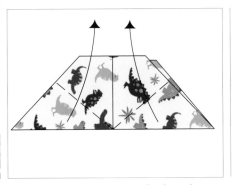

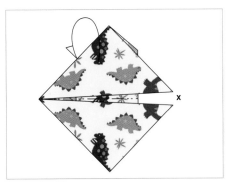

5 Fold the sharp corners up to lie along the center crease.

6 Mountain fold in half. Note the double corner at X.

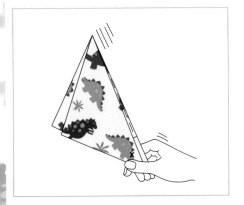

7 Hold X as shown. Bend your elbow so that the banger is behind your head, then whip it downward very quickly. The paper will unfold with a loud BANG! If it doesn't, check that you haven't held the paper upside down and try to move your arm quicker next time.

This banger has been banged! This is an origami classic, but possibly not a good project to make on long journeys...

Parrot

SKILL LEVEL

You will need

☐ 12in (30cm) square of light-weight paper

Artist's tip: Using a plastic-based wrapping paper will add strength to the model

THIS LOVELY PARROT IS PERFECT FOR PERCHING ON THE SHOULDER OF AN ASPIRING PIRATE. IT IS TOO COMPLEX FOR A BEGINNER TO CREATE, BUT WOULD MAKE A GOOD GIFT. THIS MODEL HAS SEVERAL LAYERS, SO IT MUST BE MADE FROM THIN PAPER.

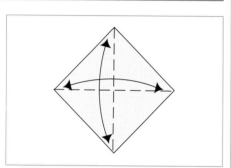

1 Crease the paper in half along both diagonals using valley folds.

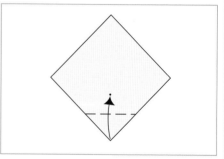

2 Fold the bottom corner to the point.

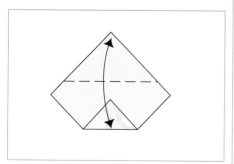

3 Fold the top corner down to meet the bottom crease.

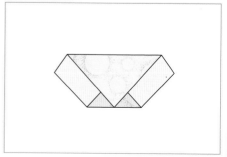

4 The first few folds dictate the final shape, so check the proportions. Unfold the top crease.

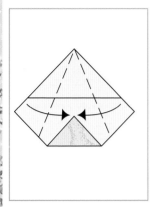

5 Fold the two sides into the center.

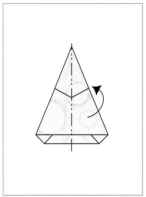

6 Mountain fold the right side behind. Rotate to the position shown in the next diagram.

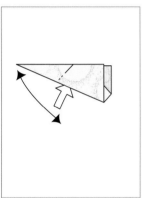

7 Reverse-fold. Unfold as shown in next diagram.

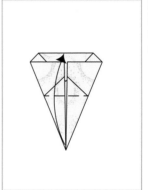

8 Fold the bottom corner to meet the top edge.

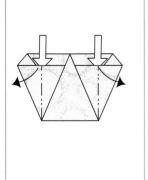

9 Open out the pockets on either side and flatten them to each side. Turn over.

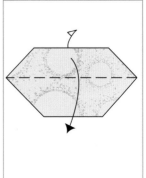

10 Fold down the upper section along the crease. Fold out the triangular flap.

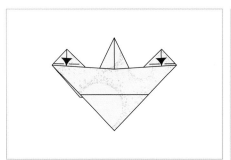

11 Fold the two small triangles inside. Turn over.

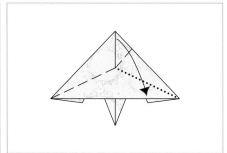

12 Fold both long edges down to the bottom edge. Flatten the point over to the right.

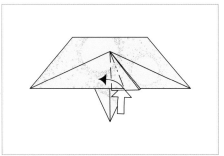

13 Lift the flap and squash flat.

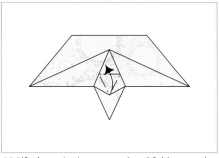

14 Lift the point just created and fold upward until the two sides come together (petal fold).

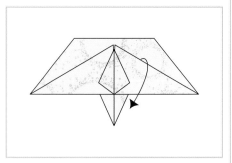

15 Fold down the flap.

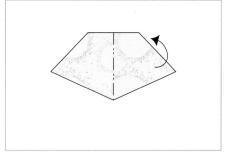

16 Mountain fold in half.

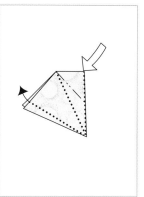

17 Pull out the inside flap. Push in the top corner as shown.

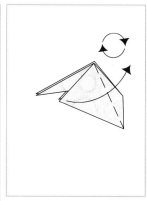

18 Fold back the flap as shown. Repeat on the other side. Rotate as shown in the next diagram.

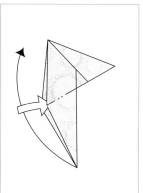

19 Reverse-fold the bottom point upward in line.

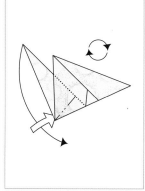

20 Reverse-fold the inner point along the line shown. Rotate as shown in the next diagram.

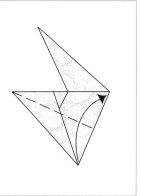

21 Fold up the flap as shown. Repeat on the other side.

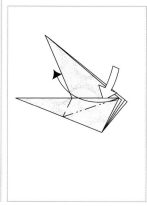

22 Fold up and open the flap. Check the next diagram to see the final position.

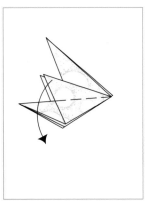

23 Fold the flap down and repeat on the opposite side to create wings.

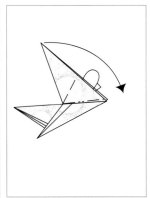

24 Crimp-fold the top point down. Rotate to the position shown in the next diagram.

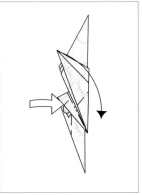

25 Open up the wings and crease as shown to hold them open. Thin the legs and tail as shown.

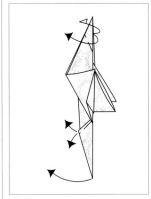

26 Reverse-fold all the layers at the top to create the head of the parrot. Open up and fold the tail forward.

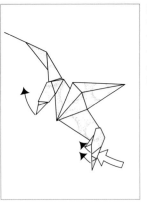

27 Reverse-fold the tip of the beak. Pleat the lower part of the beak to keep it open.

The finished parrot, ready to perch on a pirate's shoulder. For making the pirate's hat, see over the page.

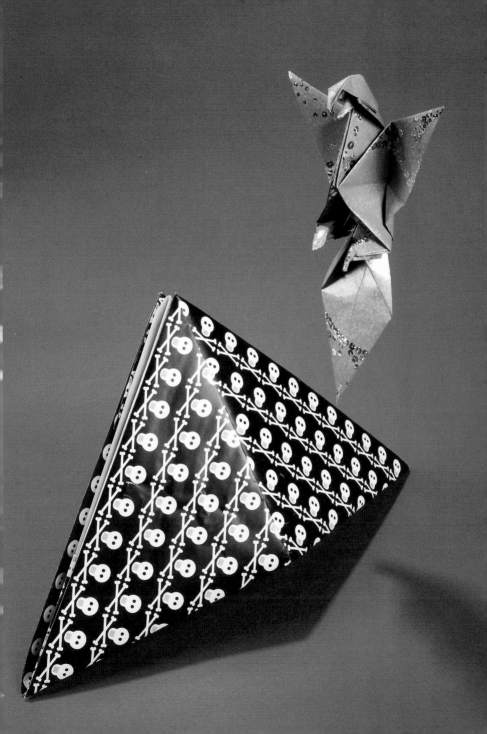

Pirate's hat

SKILL LEVEL

THIS HAT IS TRADITIONALLY MADE
FROM A LARGE SHEET OF NEWSPAPER—
BUT IT'S SO MUCH MORE EXCITING
MADE WITH PIRATICAL PAPER!

1 Fold in half from top to bottom.

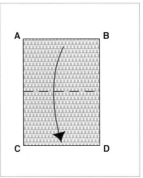

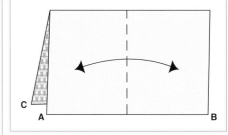

2 Fold in half, left to right. Unfold.

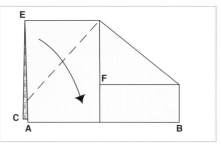

3 Fold corners E and F to the center crease.
F is shown already folded.

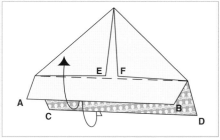

4 Fold up edge AB along the crease at the
bottom of triangles E and F. Fold up CD behind.

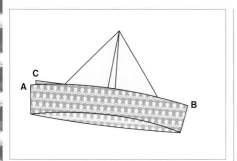

5 This makes a simple, though rather large and floppy, hat.

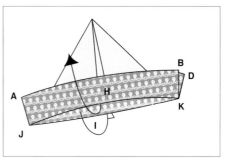

6 Hold as shown at H and I. Pull H and I apart, so that J and K come toward each other.

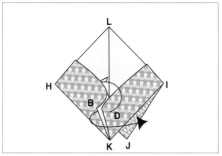

7 This makes a diamond shape. Tuck D behind B to flatten the front. Repeat behind, tucking A under C.

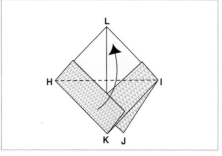

8 Fold K up to L, and behind fold J to L.

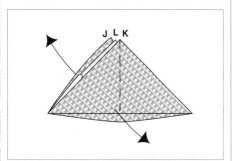

9 It should look like this—open it up to create a sturdy hat.

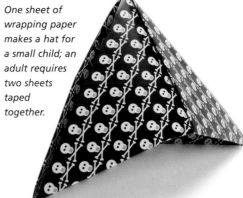

One sheet of wrapping paper makes a hat for a small child; an adult requires two sheets taped together.

Looping glider

SKILL LEVEL

You will need

☐ 10in (25cm) square of light- or medium-weight paper

Artist's tip: To fly your glider, launch upward at about 45 degrees with moderate force. If you launch slightly harder, the glider will perform aerobatics.

THIS PLANE WAS DESIGNED BY ONE OF SINGAPORE'S PREMIER FOLDERS, FRANCIS OW. ONE OR TWO OF THE MOVES ARE NOT IMMEDIATELY OBVIOUS, BUT IF YOU FOLD CAREFULLY, ALL WILL BE WELL. THE GLIDER BEGINS ITS FLIGHT WITH A LOOP THE LOOP!

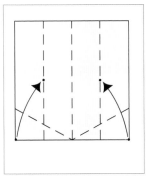

1 Valley fold the sheet into quarters. Starting at the center of the lower edge, fold corners to touch the quarter creases.

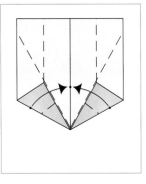

2 Take each folded edge to the center crease.

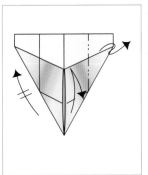

3 Now, two pre-creases: mountain fold the outer creases; valley the two existing smaller creases. This makes the next move much easier.

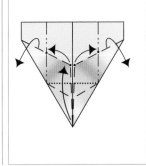

4 Unfold the mountain creases. Fold the tip inward to lie flat on the two valley creases...

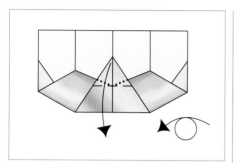

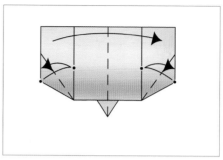

5 ...to form a new crease along the dotted line like this. Fold the triangle down as far as it will go, and turn over.

6 Reinforce the two small creases and fold in half from left to right.

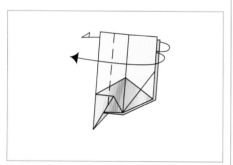

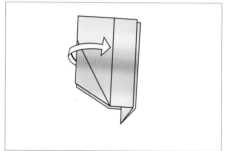

7 Fold out to form the wings. The creases begin where the side of the nose meets the horizontal edge and are parallel to the vertical edge.

8 Open out the first wing. The paper will be raised along the center. Crease where shown. Fold over the original creases to transfer the crease to the upper layer.

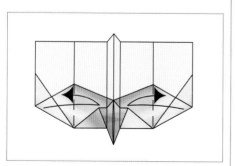

9 Raise the outer corners using the established creases to create the finished glider.

See also

Preliminary base,
page 21

Flapping bird

SKILL LEVEL

You will need

☐ 6in (15cm) square of light- or
medium-weight paper
(preliminary base)

HERE IS PERHAPS THE GREATEST OF
ALL "ACTION MODELS." THE BIRD
SHAPE IS ITSELF SATISFYING, BUT THE
WIDE, GRACEFUL ARC MADE BY THE
WINGS WHEN THEY ARE FLAPPED IS
DRAMATIC AND APPEALING.

1 Start with
the preliminary
base. With the
closed corner
at the top, fold
in the lower
front edges
to the center
crease...

2 ...like this.
Fold down the
top triangle.

3 Pull out the
side triangles.

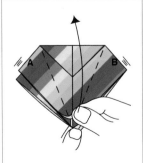

4 Take hold
of just the top
layer. Lift it
upward...

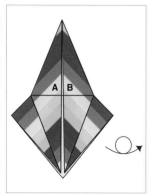

5 ...swiveling it right up and over the top edge of the paper shape. A and B will move inward. Flatten the diamond shape with strong creases. Turn over.

6 Repeat steps 1–5 on this side, to make another diamond shape to match the first. Note the loose triangle hidden between them.

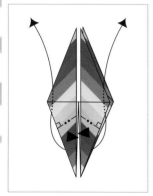

7 Reverse-fold each of the lower points, so that each reverse starts a little below the center of the diamond.

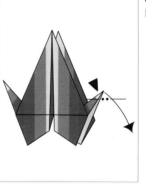

8 Reverse the head.

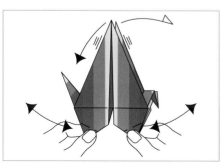

9 Hold as shown. To complete the bird, move your hands gently apart and together, apart and together, and the wings will flap!

This is a classic design, easily made from scraps of paper.

Rowing boat

SKILL LEVEL

You will need

☐ 6in (15cm) square of cardstock

THIS DESIGN BY MARTIN WALL FROM THE UK MAKES A SIMPLE SHAPE THAT IS VERY SEAWORTHY. MADE WITH CARDSTOCK THIS BOAT IS WATERPROOF ENOUGH TO RACE ON A STREAM OR RIVER, AND BIODEGRADABLE TOO, SO IT WILL NOT DAMAGE THE ENVIRONMENT.

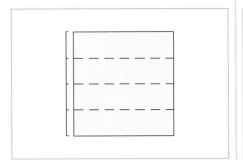

1 Valley the sheet into quarters.

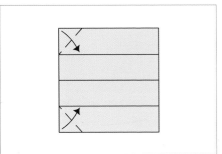

2 Turn in the left-hand corners, top and bottom.

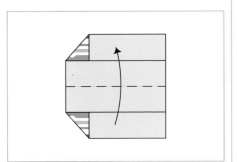

3 Fold in half.

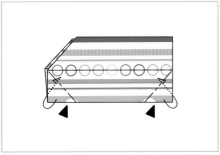

4 Reverse the bottom corners, level with the quarter crease.

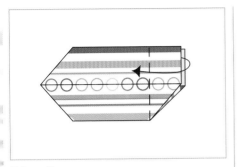

5 Open the reverse.

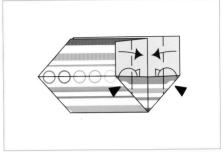

6 Reverse twice...

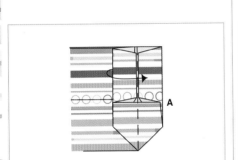

7 ...like this. Fold A across to the right.

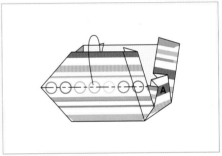

8 Tuck the nearside top quarter into the boat. Take it over the top of A, but not over the top of the reverse-fold layers at the bow (front)...

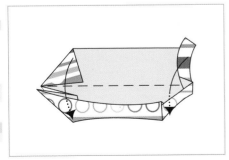

9 ...like this. Fold in the far-side layer, folding it over the reverse at the bow to close it shut.

This little flotilla could be sailed in the bathtub on a rainy day.

Puzzle

SKILL LEVEL

You will need

☐ Four 4in or 6in (10cm or 15cm) squares of light- or medium-weight paper

MANY PAPER-FOLDERS ARE ALSO INTERESTED IN MAGIC TRICKS AND GAMES THAT REQUIRE A BIT OF THOUGHT. ONE POPULAR WAY OF MAKING A PUZZLE IS TO DIVIDE A SHAPE INTO SMALLER IDENTICAL SECTIONS AND THEN CHALLENGE PEOPLE TO RECREATE THE ORIGINAL SHAPE. THESE ARE DISSECTION PUZZLES.

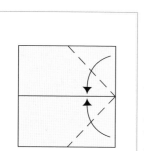

1 Start with a square, white side upward, creased in half from top to bottom. Fold the two corners shown to meet the center crease.

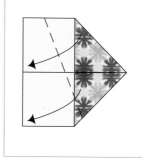

2 Take the upper right folded edge to meet the long raw edge...

3 ...like this. Unfold the last step.

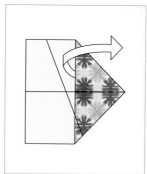

4 Unfold the upper right flap.

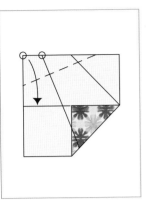

5 Make sure the corner touches the halfway crease and that the long crease will lie upon itself. The circles show reference points. Look at step 6 carefully before making this fold.

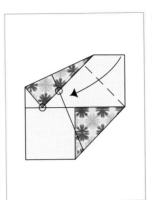

6 Refold the upper right corner on an existing crease.

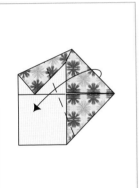

7 Again using an existing crease, fold over the lower section. Interlock the layers of paper to keep the flaps together.

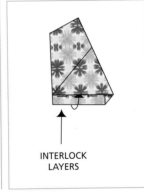

INTERLOCK
LAYERS

8 Fold over the narrow strip of white paper, tucking it underneath the upper flap. Interlock the layers at the end. The unit is complete. You will need four units in total.

One of the two solutions to the puzzle is on page 192.

Barking dog

You will need

❏ 6in (15cm) square of duo origami paper

THIS FUN AND INNOVATIVE DESIGN IS SURE TO GIVE YOU GREAT SATISFACTION. PAUL JACKSON, THE DESIGNER OF THIS UNIQUE PIECE, DISCOVERED THE ACTION AT STEP 5 BY ACCIDENT. FROM THERE, THE HEAD AND TAIL JUST FOLDED THEMSELVES.

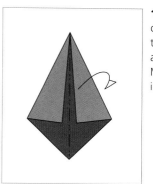

1 Fold two corners toward the center as shown. Mountain fold in half.

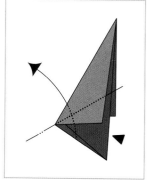

2 Reverse-fold, to the position shown in step 3.

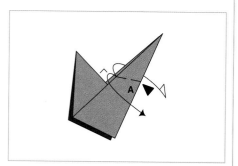

3 Outside-reverse fold, to the position shown in step 4. Note A.

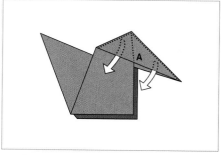

4 Pull out the internal layer at A...

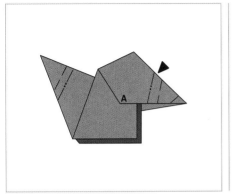

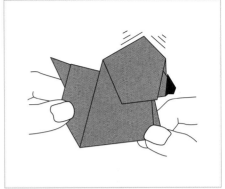

5 ...like this. Repeat behind. Make three reverse folds on the head. Pleat the tail.

6 To make him bark, hold as shown and move your left hand to the left and back again. The head will move up and down as if barking.

*Vary the creases in step 5 to
make different breeds.*

Flying saucer

You will need

❏ 6in (15cm) square of heavy-weight paper

Artist's tip: Launch the saucer like a frisbee, trying to impart as much spin as possible at the launch by "flicking" your wrist. Raise the opposite edge to your hand upward slightly.

ALTHOUGH FLYING SAUCERS ARE GENERALLY CIRCULAR, YOU CAN MAKE AN IMPRESSIVE VERSION USING A SQUARE. THIS IS EASILY CONVERTED INTO AN OCTAGON, THEN INTO A HEPTAGON AS THE PAPER IS MADE THREE-DIMENSIONAL. BECAUSE IT IS LAUNCHED WITH A SPIN, THIS DESIGN USES GYROSCOPIC PRINCIPLES.

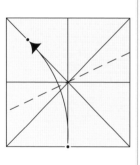

1 Crease the square in half corner to corner both ways with valleys. Make sure the crease passes through the center of the paper.

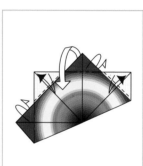

2 Take the lower center-point to lie along the upper left diagonal. Pre-crease the corners along the edges in front (valleys) and below (mountains).

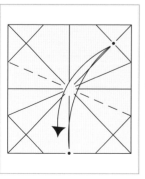

3 Open the paper back out. Repeat step 1 to the right-hand side, and unfold.

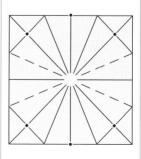

4 This is the crease pattern so far. Repeat step 1 twice more using the location marks shown to complete the radial creases.

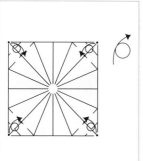

5 Fold each corner to the creases made in step 2, then over again using the crease itself. Turn the paper over.

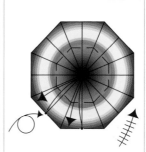

6 The paper should now be octagonal. Fold the center of each edge to the center point. Only crease between adjacent diagonals, then unfold.

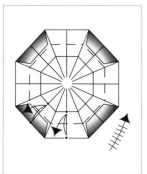

7 Turn over again. Fold each edge to the "spoke" creases you have just made, only between adjacent diagonals. Unfold.

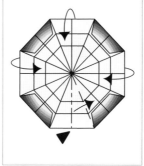

8 Make one crease into a mountain, then pleat it sideways, raising the sides of the paper to form a central hollow.

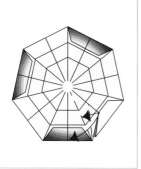

9 Lock the pleat by folding the outer edge to the diagonal, then folding over using the diagonal.

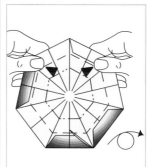

10 Lift the paper up and gently press it into shape using the creases you have made. Turn the paper over.

See also
Kite base, page 20

Woodpecker

SKILL LEVEL

You will need

❏ 6in (15cm) square of medium-weight paper (kite base)

ORIGAMI MODELS THAT HAVE SOME KIND OF MOVEMENT HAVE ALWAYS BEEN POPULAR WITH BOTH ADULTS AND CHILDREN. THIS DESIGN USES A FAMILIAR TECHNIQUE FOR CREATING MOVEMENT. IF YOU FOLD FROM STIFF PAPER, A LOUD "PECK" CAN BE HEARD.

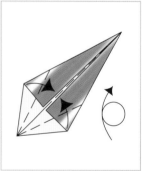

1 Begin with a kite base. Fold the short sides into the center crease. Turn over.

2 Starting at the left-hand corner, fold the right-hand edge back along itself, but only crease as far as the center. Repeat on the left-hand side.

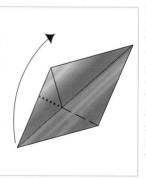

3 Turn the paper all the way around, then make the same folds at the other end. This will form a diamond-shaped crease pattern at the center.

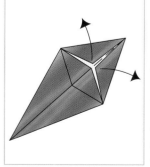

4 Turn the paper over and unfold the top two flaps at the end of the diamond base. Fold both outside corners in to meet the two inner corners and crease firmly.

 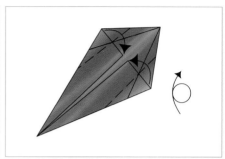

5 Pick the paper up and reinforce the diamond-shaped creases made in steps 2 and 3 so that they pass through the extra layers.

6 Make an inside reverse fold to form a beak. Turn over.

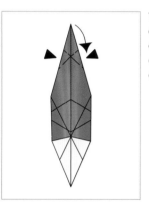

7 Fold either side of the beak downward, creasing firmly.

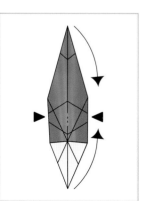

8 Hold the model by both sides and gently press together to make the completed woodpecker peck!

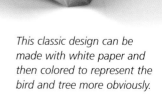

This classic design can be made with white paper and then colored to represent the bird and tree more obviously.

Pinwheel

See also
Triangle, page 24

SKILL LEVEL

You will need

❑ Triangle from Letter (A4) paper

Artist's tip: To make it spin, straighten a paper clip and insert one end through the back. Push it forward to touch the nose. Hold the protruding end of wire and push the Pinwheel through the air.

PHILIP SHEN DESIGNED THIS BEAUTIFUL, SLEEK FORM, WHICH ALMOST SEEMS TO HAVE GROWN RATHER THAN HAVING BEEN FOLDED FROM MERE PAPER. STEP 5 IS RATHER TRICKY, BUT PERSEVERE!

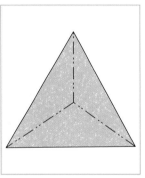

1 Crease from the corners only as far as the center point.

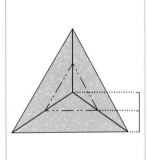

2 Make mountain creases parallel to the edges, midway between the edges and the center point. Do not crease beyond the existing creases.

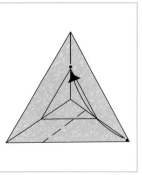

3 Fold dot to dot, but make a valley crease only where shown. Do not make it longer.

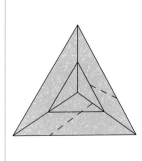

4 Repeat with the other two corners to create a symmetrical crease pattern.

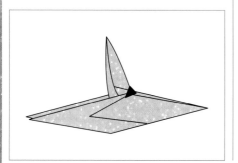

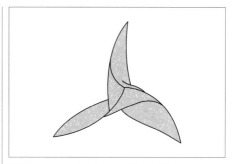

5 Strengthen all the creases, twisting the edges behind. Push in the junctions of the valley and mountain creases all at the same time.

6 This is the basic pinwheel form. Turn over.

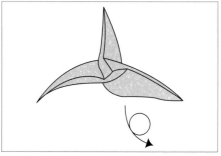

7 The center point, about which three edges rotate, stands up. Push the center point down into the body of the design to create...

8 ...a concave center, locked into shape. Turn over.

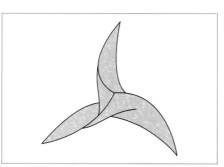

If the paper is very thin, spin the pinwheel by dropping it from a height.

9 The pinwheel is complete—a beautiful shape from only nine creases.

Ghost

SKILL LEVEL

You will need

❏ 8in (20cm) square of light- or medium-weight paper

SEVERAL GHOSTS OF VARYING SIZES COULD BE SUSPENDED ON A THREAD AND DISPLAYED IN WINDOWS FOR HALLOWEEN, OR SMALLER ONES CAN BE USED TO DECORATE INVITATION CARDS TO A "TRICK OR TREAT" PARTY. THE DRAWN EYES ARE A CHEAT, PERHAPS, BUT THERE'S NO DOUBT THAT THEY PROVIDE A SUITABLY GHOULISH EFFECT!

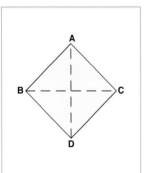

1 Crease and unfold both diagonals as valleys.

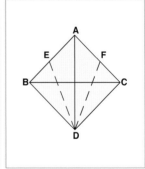

2 Fold edges DB and DC to center crease DA. Unfold.

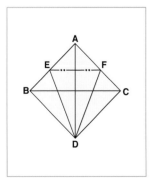

3 Connect E and F with a mountain fold. Unfold.

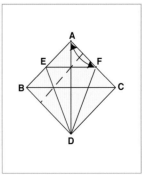

4 Fold A to F. Unfold.

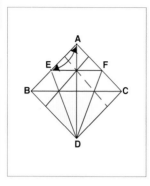

5 Fold A to E. Unfold.

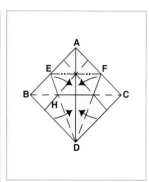

6 Carefully collapse along the marked creases. Bring E and F into the center. Let A swing down to touch E. Pull B and C downward. Look at step 7.

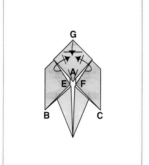

7 Fold in the diagonal edges above EF to the center crease, then fold down the top corner, G, on top.

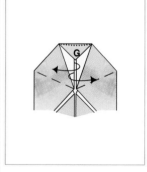

8 Unfold the side triangles, leaving the top corner folded down.

9 Pick up the single-layer corner A, and swivel it up and over the top edge of the paper.

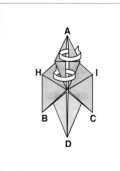

10 Unfold AEF almost to a flat sheet, swinging edges AE and AF behind to touch G (miss this step out if using single-sided paper)...

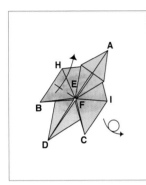

11 ...like this. Note the large triangle now below A. Fold up corner B. Turn over.

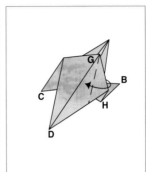

12 Fold in edge GH, not quite as far as the center crease.

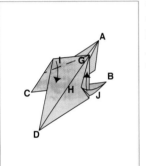

13 Collapse flat the triangle between H and J. Fold in edge GI, as shown.

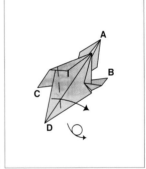

14 Fold out D to the right. Turn over.

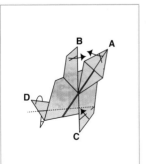

15 Fold A out to the left. Fold in B and C. Pleat D downward.

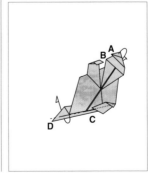

16 Narrow A. Pleat D back upward. Draw in the eyes with a black marker pen.

CHRISTMAS ORIGAMI

Homemade Christmas decorations are traditionally brought
home from school by children, and then brought out with pride
by mothers to embarrass their teenagers in later years. The
decorations shown here are simple and stylish and can be made
by the whole family for later enjoyment. Paper decorations are
particularly suitable for those with young children or animals, as
less injury can result from chewing on a paper bauble, and they
are much more likely to bounce!

Bauble

You will need

❑ 12in x 3in (30cm x 7.5cm) of light-weight paper or foil

Artist's tip: In places where you need to create accurate creases, use a clean pair of tweezers or your thumbnail and a flat surface. Rough surfaces or a ragged nail will damage foils and glossy papers.

THIS DESIGN WORKS BEST WHEN MADE WITH SHINY, UNPATTERNED PAPER. TO THE BEHOLDER, IT APPEARS HIGHLY COMPLEX, BUT IT IS ACTUALLY A SIMPLE CREASE PATTERN REPEATED MANY TIMES ALONG THE PAPER. THE SECRET OF ITS SUCCESS IS TO CREASE ACCURATELY.

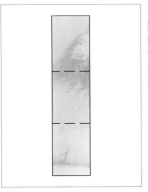

1 With the paper right-side up, valley fold twice to form three equal sections.

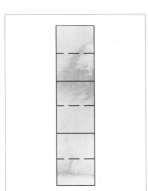

2 Make valley folds midway between each section, creating six equal divisions.

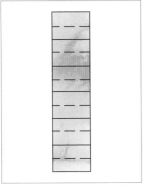

3 Make valley folds midway between the existing creases, creating 12 equal divisions.

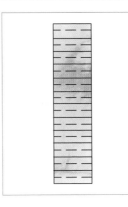

4 Make valley folds midway between each of the existing creases, creating 24 equal divisions. Keep the folds accurate.

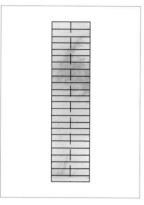

5 Fold the sheet in half along its length. Unfold.

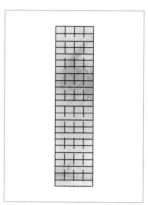

6 Fold the sides into the middle of the sheet, creasing right along its length. Unfold.

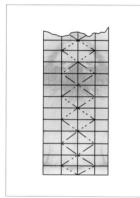

7 Look at the crease pattern so far. All the existing creases are valleys, while the new ones will be mountains.

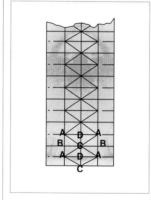

8 Now make careful diagonal mountain folds across the middle, as shown, making sure your folds exactly connect at the intersections of existing creases.

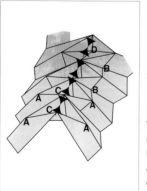

9 Along the outer-edge sections, re-crease alternate valleys. This produces a pleated effect, with diamonds across the middle. Locate As, Bs, Cs, and Ds.

10 Squeeze the pleats together so that the side and end points (C and A) of the diamonds rise up, and the mid-points (D) of the diamonds and pleats (B) cave in.

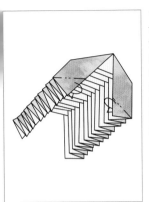

11 Press firmly to reinforce all the creases, and then turn over. Mountain fold the single-layer corners inside at both the front ends.

12 Valley fold the double-layer corners on the inside edges, as shown.

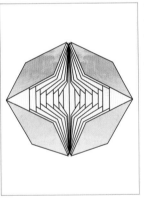

13 Repeat all the way down the row of pleats, neatly folding in each corner in turn.

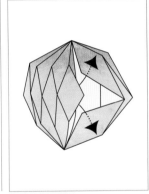

14 Bring the ends around and together to form a sphere. Tuck the left-hand edge under the right, as shown, locking the bauble.

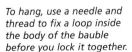

To hang, use a needle and thread to fix a loop inside the body of the bauble before you lock it together.

Four-piece star

SKILL LEVEL

You will need

❏ 4in x 6in (10cm x 15cm) squares of medium-weight paper

ONE OF THE BEST WAYS TO FORM GEOMETRIC SHAPES IS TO FOLD A NUMBER OF SIMPLE SHAPES THAT CAN INTERLOCK. THIS IS COMMONLY KNOWN AS "MODULAR ORIGAMI." THE FOUR-PIECE STAR IS A SIMPLE EXAMPLE OF THIS KIND OF FOLDING, AND IS AN IDEAL PROJECT FOR THE BEGINNER.

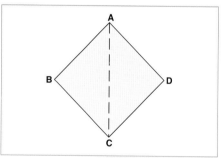

1 Fold B over to D. Crease and unfold.

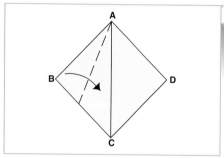

2 Fold in edge AB to lie along crease AC.

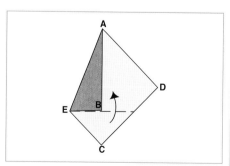

3 Fold up C along a crease that follows edge EB, covering B.

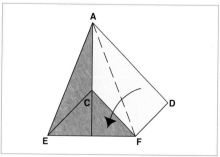

4 Fold in edge AD to the center so that it half-covers C.

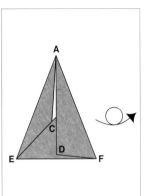

5 The paper now looks like this. Turn over.

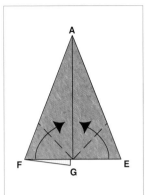

6 Fold in F and E to lie along crease AG.

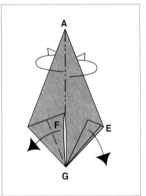

7 Fold F and E back out to the just-formed sloping edges that meet at G. E is shown already folded. Keep the folds neat at G.

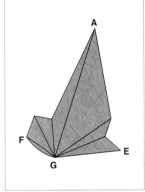

8 Unfold the last two steps so it looks like this. This is one point of the star. Make three more sections in the same way as the first.

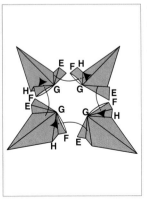

9 Tuck corner E of one section in between the layers of another at F, until E touches H and the two Gs touch. The mountain and valley creases should line up where they overlap.

This star is made from "stacks" of coordinating Christmas papers.

Placecard

You will need

- ❏ 5in x 4in (13cm x 10cm) thin patterned card
- ❏ Letter-size (A4) sheet of white card
- ❏ Scissors
- ❏ Colored pens

A FINISHING TOUCH TO A PLACE SETTING IS TO MAKE A CARD THAT CARRIES THE NAME OF THE GUEST WHO IS TO SIT THERE. USE PATTERNED PAPERS, OR GLUE TINY ORIGAMI MODELS TO THE SIDE TO FIT YOUR THEME.

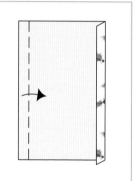

1 Fold in about ⅓in (1cm) along the longer edges. The right-hand side is shown already folded.

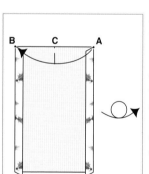

2 Bring top corners A and B together and pinch to locate the middle of the top edge (C). Do not make a long crease. Unfold and turn over.

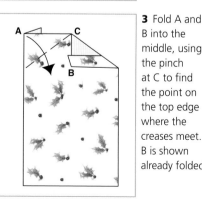

3 Fold A and B into the middle, using the pinch at C to find the point on the top edge where the creases meet. B is shown already folded.

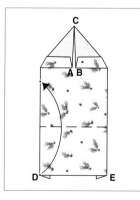

4 Fold up D and E to lie just below the base of the triangle. The exact placement is unimportant.

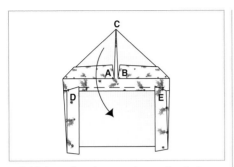

5 Fold down C and crease along a line just above DE.

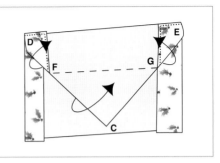

6 Flip loose corners D and E to the front, trapping the corners of the large C triangle behind them. Make a valley crease between F and G, lifting corner C.

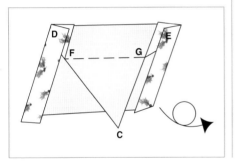

7 This is the back of the placecard, with C forming a stand. Turn over.

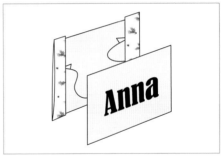

8 Write your guest's name on the tag using colored pens.

To create models to attach to the side of the placecard, try a 3in (7.5cm) square for size, but make sure you use light-weight paper.

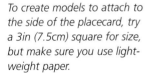

See also
Triangle, page 24

Six-point star

SKILL LEVEL

ONE OF THE SIMPLEST AND MOST
ATTRACTIVE OF ALL FOLDED
DECORATIONS, THE SIX-POINT STAR USES
THE MOST BASIC FOLDING TECHNIQUES.
USING DUO PAPER WILL CREATE A STAR
THAT IS EQUALLY ATTRACTIVE FROM
EITHER SIDE, WHILE USING TEXTURED
PAPER (AS SHOWN) GIVES A LUXURIOUS
FEEL TO THIS SIMPLE DECORATION.

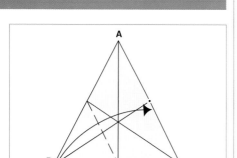

1 Start with a triangle. Fold B across to the
opposite edge.

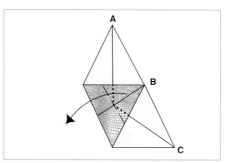

2 Fold B back along a crease that passes over
the center of the triangle.

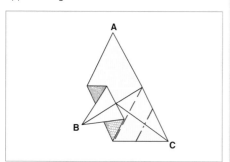

3 Repeat steps 1 and 2 for C.

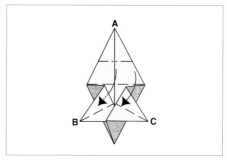

4 Repeat steps 1 and 2 for A. Tuck the left-
hand part of the pleat under B to lock A, B, and
C together in a symmetrical pattern...

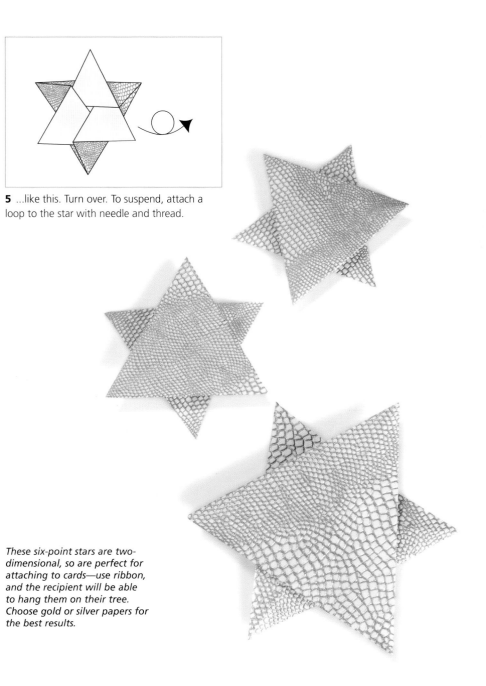

5 ...like this. Turn over. To suspend, attach a loop to the star with needle and thread.

These six-point stars are two-dimensional, so are perfect for attaching to cards—use ribbon, and the recipient will be able to hang them on their tree. Choose gold or silver papers for the best results.

Angel

▲▲▲
SKILL LEVEL

THIS ELEGANT, ABSTRACT DESIGN IS VERY DIFFERENT FROM THE MORE CONVENTIONALLY SHAPED ANIMAL DESIGNS ELSEWHERE IN THE BOOK. IT CAPTURES THE LIKENESS OF THE ANGEL WITH ONLY A FEW FOLDS; THIS PURITY CAN BE ENHANCED BY THE USE OF SEMI-TRANSPARENT JAPANESE PAPER.

You will need

❏ Sheet of light- or medium-weight letter paper (A4)

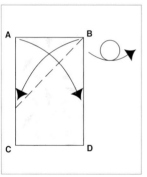

1 Fold A over to lie on edge BD. Unfold. Fold B over to lie on edge AC. Crease, unfold, and turn over.

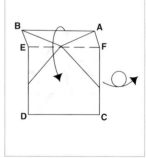

2 Make a horizontal valley fold that passes through the center-point of the mountain "cross." Turn back over.

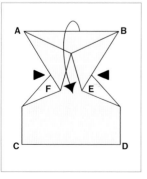

3 Holding the sides of the paper at E and F, let A and B rise up as the sides are brought inward...

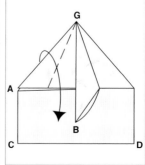

4 Imagine a center crease from the top point (G) down the middle of the paper. Fold in A and B to lie along the imaginary crease. Keep it neat at G.

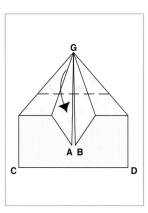

5 Fold G down to AB. Crease firmly.

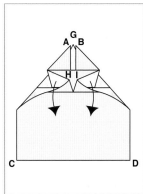

6 Hold G, A, and B, and swing them back up to where G used to be. Flatten the paper to form triangles H and I. Hold the paper with your left hand at H, and...

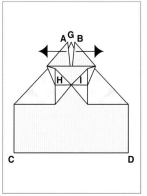

7 ...pull B and A away from G (see the next drawing to check the new position). Flatten and crease. Turn over.

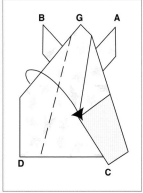

8 Fold in the sides so that they overlap in the center (see next step). Note that they do not quite meet at G. C has already been folded.

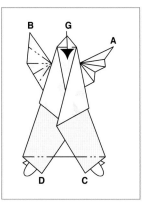

9 Tuck D and C behind. Fold down G. Carefully pleat the wings as shown.

The Angel has a pocket on the back which can be used to attach it securely to the top of your tree; alternatively, it can be attached to a handmade card.

Man in the Moon

You will need

❏ 6in (15cm) square of medium-weight paper

THIS DESIGN LOOKS VERY ATTRACTIVE ON A GREETINGS CARD OR AS A HANGING DECORATION, SUSPENDED ON A LENGTH OF THREAD. WATCH OUT THOUGH: YOU MUST MAKE THE REVERSE FOLDS VERY CAREFULLY OR THE PROPORTIONS OF THE FACE WILL DISTORT.

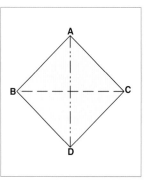

1 Crease BC as a valley and AD as a mountain. Unfold both.

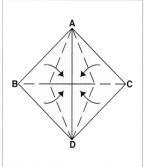

2 Fold edges AB and AC to crease AD, creasing down from A only as far as crease BC. Repeat for the bottom half. Collapse the paper...

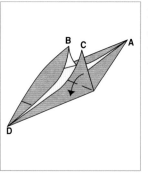

3 ...like this. The paper will not lie flat. Flatten C toward D.

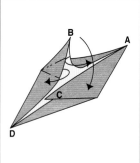

4 Pull B open and squash flat...

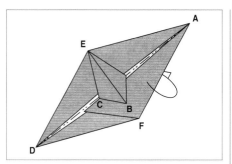

5 ...like this. Fold F behind to E. Rotate the paper to look like step 6.

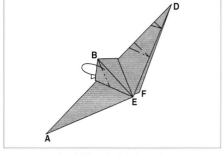

6 Narrow B by folding behind. Make two sets of crimp folds on the upper triangle. Make the larger pair first, reverse-folding along the mountain crease, then back along the valley.

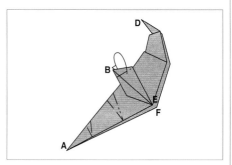

7 Fold B behind, as shown. Make two more sets of crimp folds on the lower triangle as described above, the larger set first.

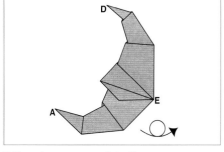

8 The crimps are complete. Turn over.

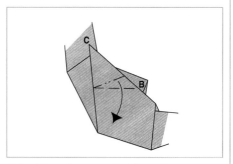

9 Pleat C as shown, so that it creates...

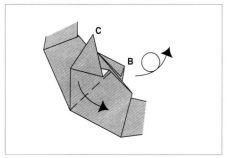

10 ...this shape. Fold C downward. Turn over.

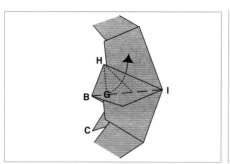

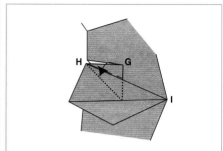

11 Pull out corner G with a reverse fold, so that G becomes visible above edge HI.

12 Pull down the top layer of edge HG, partly squashing G open to form an eye...

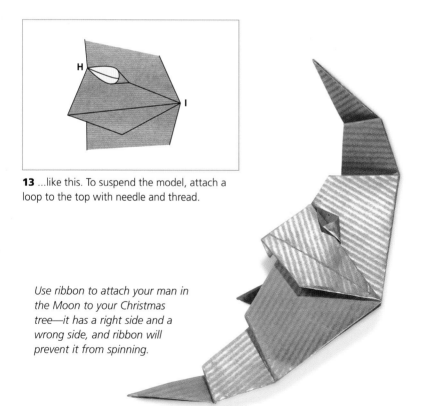

13 ...like this. To suspend the model, attach a loop to the top with needle and thread.

Use ribbon to attach your man in the Moon to your Christmas tree—it has a right side and a wrong side, and ribbon will prevent it from spinning.

FOLDER'S HEAVEN

This chapter is made up of models that do not look particularly exciting, but are highly enjoyable to fold. Each one has a trick to it, or a special move that looks rather like magic. Practice these models until you can make the special moves smoothly, then you can astonish all your friends!

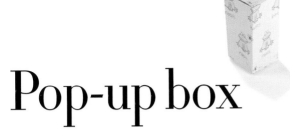

Pop-up box

SKILL LEVEL

<table>
<tr><td>

You will need

❏ 12in (30cm) square of light- to medium-weight paper

</td><td>

THIS IS AN EXTREME EXAMPLE OF FOLDING FOR FOLDING'S SAKE. THE DESIGN, BY ERIC KENNEWAY OF THE UK, IS RATHER UNSPECTACULAR TO BEHOLD WHEN COMPLETE, BUT THE FOLDING PROCESS IS HIGHLY ENJOYABLE, AND THE FINAL MOVE IS PURE MAGIC.

</td></tr>
</table>

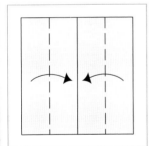

1 Valley fold the edges to the center crease.

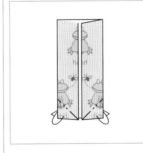

2 Mountain fold the bottom corners behind.

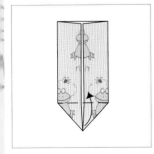

3 Fold up the triangle.

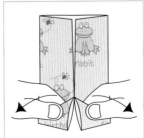

4 Moisten your fingers for a good grip and hold as shown. Pull the outer layers, sliding them out to the sides...

5 ...like this. Flatten the paper by bringing the corners together.

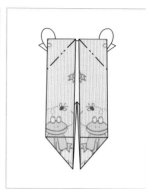

6 The move is complete. Repeat steps 2–5 at the top.

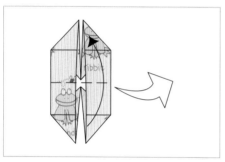

7 Fold in half.

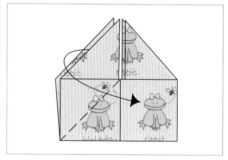

8 Fold across to the right.

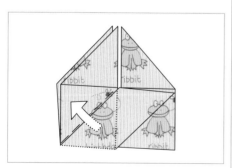

9 Pull out the hidden corner.

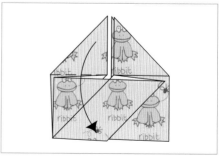

10 Fold down the triangle.

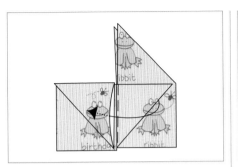

11 Tuck the loose triangle right inside the pocket. Keep it neat.

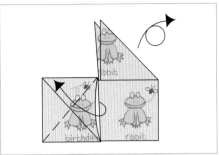

12 Fold the loose corner up and to the left. Turn over.

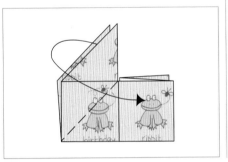

13 Repeat steps 8–12 on this side.

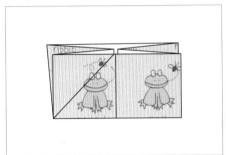

14 Creasing is complete.

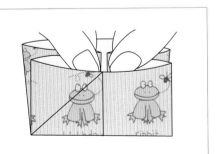

15 Hold as shown and pull the central flaps upward and outward to form the completed model.

Funky wrapping papers make these boxes more exciting!

Snap hexahedron

You will need

☐ 7in (17.5cm) square of light- or medium-weight paper (folded to create a 4 x 4 grid by creasing into quarters horizontally and vertically; then cut down to leave a 3 x 3 grid)

HEXAHEDRONS ARE COMMON IN ORIGAMI. ANY SIX-SIDED STRUCTURE IS CALLED A HEXAHEDRON AND THOSE WITH ALL SIDES EQUAL ARE FURTHER CATEGORIZED AS CUBES. THIS DESIGN BY EDWIN CORRIE FROM THE UK IS ONE OF THE SIMPLEST, AND FEATURES A "SNAP" INTO SHAPE, WHICH MAKES IT EXTREMELY INTERESTING TO FOLD.

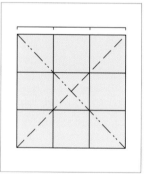

1 Fold one diagonal as a mountain and the other diagonal as a valley.

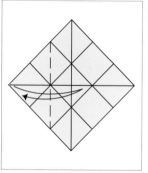

2 Fold dot to dot. Unfold.

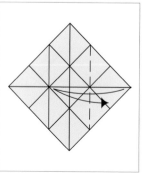

3 Similarly, fold dot to dot the other way. Unfold.

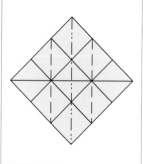

4 Pleat as shown (see next step).

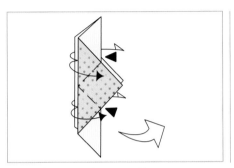

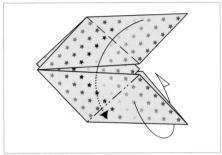

5 Outside-reverse the top and bottom corners (see next step).

6 Valley fold the top corner into the pocket formed by the lower outside-reverse fold. Then, mountain the lower corner into the upper outside-reverse fold, behind.

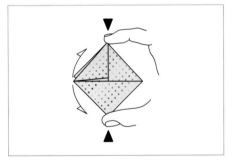

7 Hold as shown and squeeze. The left-hand corners will separate to create a third edge around the middle, forming a three-dimensional hexahedron shape.

Snap hexahedrons make beautiful hanging Christmas decorations, if pure folding enjoyment is not enough!

Modular ball

See also

Fuse box, page 46

SKILL LEVEL

You will need

❑ Six 3in x 1.5in (8cm x 4cm) strips of light- or medium-weight paper

Artist's tip: For three-dimensional origami, wrapping papers may not be stiff enough to maintain the structure—use spray mount to attach it to ordinary letter paper (A4) before you cut to the right size.

TOMOKO FUSE IS WELL-KNOWN FOR HER FANTASTIC MODULAR APPROACH TO ORIGAMI. THIS BALL HAS NO REAL PURPOSE, BUT ITS INTRICATE DESIGN IS A GOOD INTRODUCTION TO THE WORLD OF MODULAR STRUCTURES. BY PLAYING WITH THIS SHAPE, YOU WILL BE ABLE TO CREATE YOUR OWN.

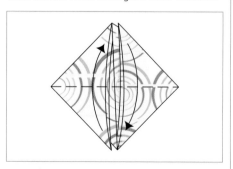

1 Fold up the bottom left-hand corner, and fold down the top right-hand corner. Always fold these corners when folding the other modules.

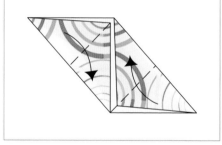

2 Fold each triangle in half...

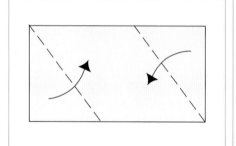

3 ...and again.

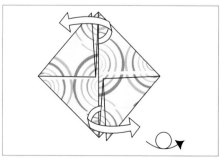

4 Unfold each side a little. Turn over.

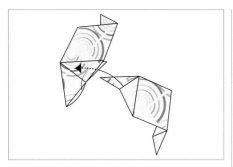

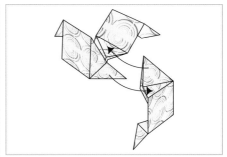

5 The finished module. Make five more. All six should be identical—no mirror images.

6 Tuck a 45-degree corner on one module, into the pocket of another...

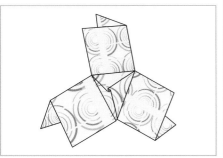

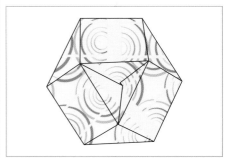

7 ...like this. Feed in a third module, tucking its 45-degree corner into the pocket of the top module, while tucking the corner of the left-hand module into the pocket of the third module.

8 Note how every module tucks into the pocket of the next, to form a well-locked inverted pyramid. Lock in the other three modules to complete the design.

Trying to make the modules fit inside one another can be a frustrating process, but persevere.

Paper mosaic

SKILL LEVEL

You will need

❏ Multiple 1.5in (4cm) square tiles in light-weight paper

THESE LITTLE TILES CAN BE LINKED TOGETHER TO FORM ALL KINDS OF PATTERNS AND WILL MAKE ATTRACTIVE CARDS AND PAPER MOSAICS. ALTHOUGH THESE LITTLE TILES DON'T HAVE MUCH OF A PURPOSE, THEY ARE VERY USEFUL FOR HONING YOUR SKILLS AND IMPROVING YOUR ACCURACY.

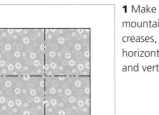

1 Make central mountain creases, horizontally and vertically.

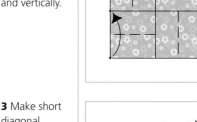

2 Fold the bottom edge of the paper dot to dot, but only crease from the left-hand edge into the center. Do this with all the other edges.

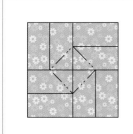

3 Make short diagonal mountain creases connecting the points where the step 1 and 2 creases meet. Strengthen all creases.

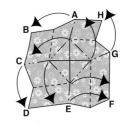

4 Pinch the short mountain creases at A, C, E, and G and fold them over to corners B, D, F, and H along the step 2 creases.

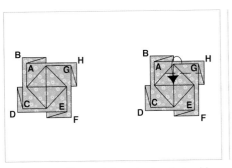 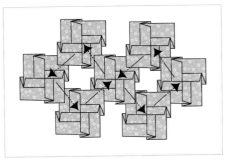

5 The center diamond shape in step 4 should have twisted counter-clockwise. This step shows the flattened paper. Bring the folded edge at the top of the paper (G) down to the center.

6 Repeat with the three other folded edges to make the complete unit. Make as many as you need and interlock them as shown.

This is a pattern of nine tiles like the one shown above, made from flowery duo paper.

Stretch wall

SKILL LEVEL

You will need

❏ 12in (30cm) square of cardstock

THIS DESIGN BY YOSHIHIDE MOMOTANI OF JAPAN IS ASTONISHING, AS IT CAN EXPAND AND COLLAPSE. THE DESIGN IS NOT DIFFICULT TO FOLLOW, BUT IT IS TIME-CONSUMING AND REQUIRES PATIENCE. THE FINAL "UNPICKING" OF THE EDGES IN STEPS 16–18 IS A VERY PRETTY AND DRAMATIC CONCLUSION.

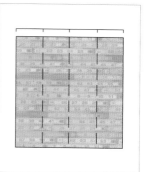

1 Crease accurate quarters, all valleys.

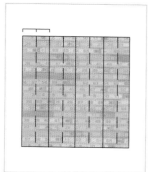

2 Crease accurate eighths, all valleys.

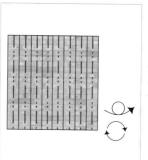

3 Place mountains midway between the valleys. Turn over and rotate the paper.

4 Check that the top crease is a valley (if it isn't, turn the paper over so that it is).

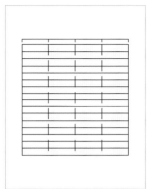

5 Repeat steps 1–3, creasing valleys as quarters and eighths, then mountains in between...

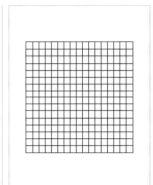

6 ...to make this grid.

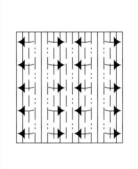

7 Make pleats where shown...

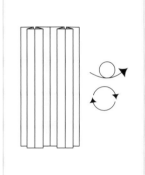

8 ...like this. Turn the paper over and rotate.

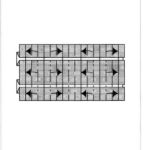

9 Pleat again.

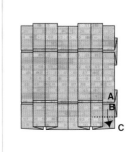

10 The pleats are complete. Note A, B, and C. Fold so the lower pleat swivels downward...

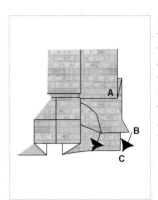

11 ...like this. Note the diagonal crease that has to be made beneath the vertical pleat to accommodate the swivel.

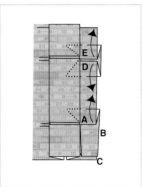

12 Repeat the swivel with A, D, and E.

13 Repeat down the center, swiveling the pleat upward to lie level with the top edge.

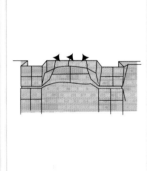

14 As before, diagonal creases need to be made beneath the vertical pleats; this time, one at each end of the swivel.

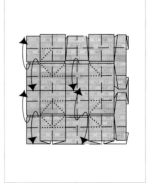

15 The swivel is done. Repeat three more times down the center, and four times down the left-hand edge.

16 Note FG and HI. Fold edge GH across to the right, so that G separates from F and H separates from I. Pull out the paper beneath F and I, so that edge GH can flatten...

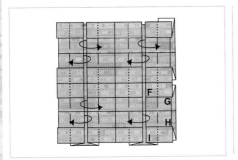

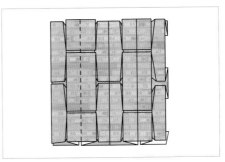

17 ...like this. Pull out the paper beneath F and I, so that edge GH can flatten to the right...

18 ...like this. Repeat, "unbuttoning" more edges to reveal a regular brick pattern.

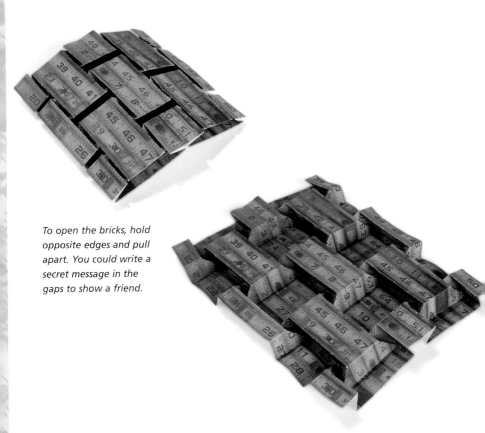

To open the bricks, hold opposite edges and pull apart. You could write a secret message in the gaps to show a friend.

Cube

SKILL LEVEL

You will need

❑ 8in (20cm) square of medium-weight paper

THE END PRODUCT OF THIS ISN'T PARTICULARLY EXCITING, BUT ITS CREATOR, SHUZO FUJIMOTO OF JAPAN HAS COME UP WITH ONE OF THE MOST ASTONISHING MOVES IN ORIGAMI FOR STEP 5; MAKE SURE YOU GET STEP 2 RIGHT, OR THE CUBE WON'T FORM.

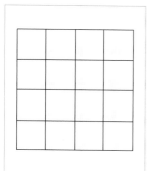

1 Carefully divide the paper into quarters, horizontally and vertically, to create 16 squares.

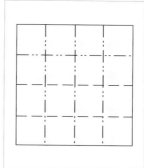

2 Re-crease the creases to look like the pattern of mountains and valleys shown here.

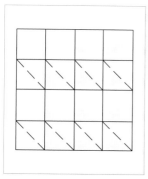

3 Add eight short diagonals. Be precise.

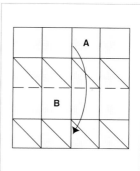

4 Fold in half. Note squares A and B.

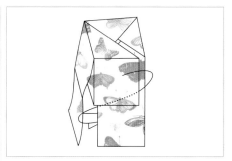

5 Hold as shown. Note square A at the front and B behind. Slide A up and to the left, so it exactly covers B.

6 The paper will curl into a cube form. All the creases must form cleanly and simultaneously. Tuck the front square inside to lock the top.

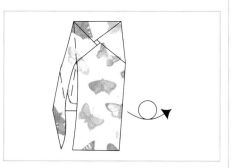

7 Turn over.

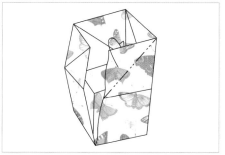

8 Fold in the corner.

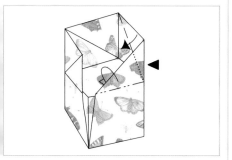

9 Push in the next corner to form part of the lid.

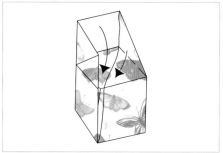

10 Push in the next corner...

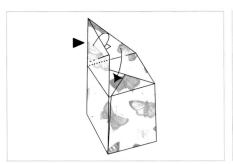

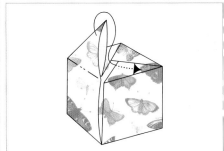

11 ...and the next.

12 Tuck the triangle inside the cube to lock the top.

Once you've made one of these cubes, you'll be fascinated... make sure you have a set of attractive papers on hand so you can make some more!

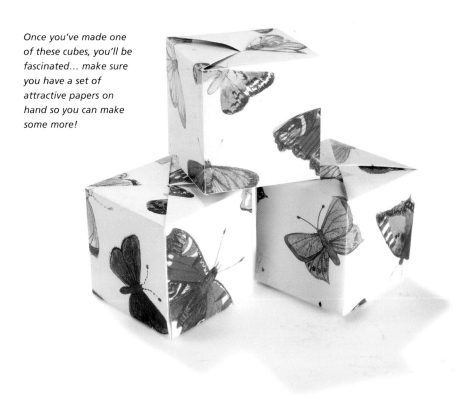

Un-unfoldable box

SKILL LEVEL

You will need

❑ 12in (30cm) square of cardstock

THIS BOX BY ED SULLIVAN OF THE USA IS PARTICULARLY PLAIN. HOWEVER, THE REMARKABLE THING ABOUT THIS DESIGN IS THAT IT CANNOT BE UNFOLDED ONCE CREATED. IT IS UNIQUE IN ORIGAMI, AND IS SURE TO PROVE A FAVORITE OF ANYONE WHO MAKES IT.

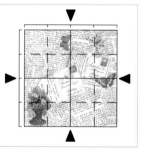

1 Pinch the mid-points of the four edges. Use them as a guide to make four valley creases along the horizontal and vertical quarter marks.

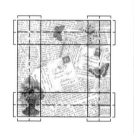

2 Make mountain folds midway between the valley quarters and the edges.

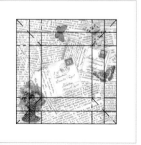

3 Form valley diagonals at the corners and fold to create a box with triangular flaps.

4 Point two flaps to the left and two to the right. Fold the triangles in half by turning the loose corners inside.

5 Fold the triangles to the inside, flat against the box.

6 Collapse the box, bringing A down to C and B down to D.

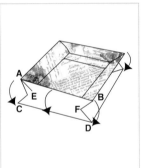

7 Move E and F toward the center of the front edge. Repeat behind.

8 This is the shape fully collapsed. Note E and F.

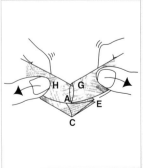

9 Hold corner AC as shown. Pull your hands gently apart and H will slide away from G. Keep pulling...

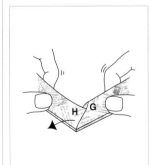

10 ...until the corner is fully formed. Repeat for the other corners of the box.

magic \'maj-ik\ n [ME
magike, fem. of *magique*
sorcerer, of Iranian orig
use of means (as cha
power over natural fo
extraordinary powe
source **b** : somethi
3 : the art of pro
2magic *adj* **1** : of
natural

in·spi·ra·tion
ciated with inspiration
in·spire \in\ *vb* [ME inspiren, fr. MF
spirare to breathe — more at S
blow into or upon **b** archaic
3 a : to influence, m
: to exert
c : AFFECT
CREATE

cre·a·tion
bringing
making, in

Fräulein
Emilie Feigl
W...

MF *magiq*
magic

Index

MAIN REFERENCES TO FOLDS, BASES, AND
PAPER TYPES ARE INDICATED IN BOLD TYPE.

Key to symbols

This system of arrows and patterns describes every design instruction used in the book. Keep this page open as you work through the projects, or until you become more familiar with these universally-recognized folding symbols.

Each model has a skill rating, indicated by the above symbols. Models with one "kite" use only one or two types of fold and are for beginner artists. Intermediate artists should attempt models with 2, 3, or 4 "kites." Projects marked with five "kites" are for advanced artists only.

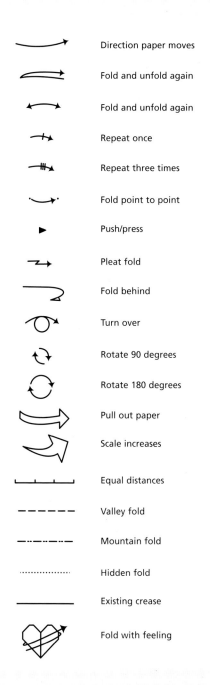

Direction paper moves

Fold and unfold again

Fold and unfold again

Repeat once

Repeat three times

Fold point to point

Push/press

Pleat fold

Fold behind

Turn over

Rotate 90 degrees

Rotate 180 degrees

Pull out paper

Scale increases

Equal distances

Valley fold

Mountain fold

Hidden fold

Existing crease

Fold with feeling

Origami bases

LEARN THESE THREE TRADITIONAL ORIGAMI BASES AND YOU WILL BE ABLE TO MAKE ANY OF THE MODELS IN THIS BOOK.

KITE BASE

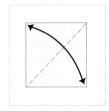 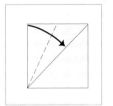  

PRELIMINARY BASE

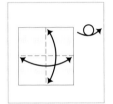 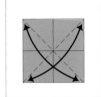 

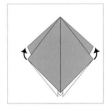 

WATERBOMB BASE

 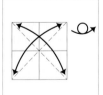 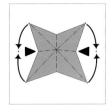 

Credits

Thanks to Nick Robinson for the use of his dollar bill rhino model, page 13.

Author's dedication
KR—I should have followed your advice and done this ages ago! Chris, thanks for everything x

ANSWER
Here is one of the two answers to the Puzzle project, which you will find on pages 138–139.